THE VACATION CHURCH SCHOOL
IN CHRISTIAN EDUCATION

THE COOPERATIVE SERIES
Leadership Training Texts

Many thousands of lay workers in Protestant churches attend interdenominational leadership education schools each year. It is essential that the courses offered and the text materials used be acceptable to the many varieties of Protestant groups found in our American communities.

The Cooperative Series of leadership education textbooks are produced to meet that need. They are planned by the Division of Christian Education of the National Council of the Churches of Christ in the U.S.A., representing thirty-nine Protestant denominations. The Cooperative Publication Association, an interdenominational group of denominational editors and publishers, selects the writers and provides editorial supervision to insure sound educational values, practical usefulness, and interdenominational approval and acceptance.

ELSIE MILLER BUTT

THE
Vacation Church School
IN
Christian Education

PUBLISHED FOR

The Cooperative Publication Association

BY

A B I N G D O N P R E S S
NEW YORK   •   NASHVILLE

THE VACATION CHURCH SCHOOL IN CHRISTIAN EDUCATION

Copyright © MCMLVII by Abingdon Press

Library of Congress Catalog Card Number: 57-6754

B

SET UP, PRINTED, AND BOUND BY THE PARTHENON PRESS, AT NASHVILLE, TENNESSEE, UNITED STATES OF AMERICA

Dedicated

To the memory of a Christian minister
who prized the vacation church school
as a means of serving boys and girls

CONTENTS

PART I

THE VACATION CHURCH SCHOOL PICTURE

Going to vacation church school may be the beginning of a continuing church experience.

What Is the Vacation Church School?

THE MEDITATIONS OF ONE WHO CARES ABOUT THE CHRISTIAN GROWTH OF BOYS AND GIRLS

IT IS EIGHT O'CLOCK ON A SUMMER WEEKDAY MORNING, AND the doors of the Protestant church stand open. One might suppose they are open to let in the cool morning air, but several adults and many boys and girls are going in that direction. Cars, driven by mothers, come filled with children and older boys and girls.

From outside observation one can gather considerable information about the nature of this vacation church school. The sign in front of the church announces that the boys and girls of the community are welcome. A local church's vacation school is usually open to everyone whether or not he is a member of the sponsoring church. This one may even be an interdenominational co-operative vacation church school giving boys and girls an opportunity to widen their experiences across denominational lines.

There are no doubt boys and girls going into that vacation church school who do not go anywhere to church on Sundays. But since playmates go, why not go along? Perhaps this will be the beginning of continuing church experiences. One hopes so.

This vacation church school lasts several weeks. Three hours a day for five days a week are fifteen hours a week. One month of this exceeds what we have in a whole year in many church schools. No wonder this church has a vacation school! A smart idea, this is, using the summer which is sometimes a long annual vacuum in the lives of boys and girls with public schools closed, music teachers on vacation, and unfortunately, many church schools closed,

11

Oscar J. Rumpf

Vacation church school meets the needs of boys and girls.

too. Our homes have so many gadgets that many boys and girls have little work to do there. The summer, so eagerly anticipated, becomes boring for many children about a week after school closes. Yes, a need is met in their lives by the church that plans for a vacation church school.

Vacation! The word has an appealing sound. But can it be a vacation and be a school, too? At various times during the morning I see different groups coming outdoors to play, or perhaps to plant seeds in a flower bed as a group of four- and five-year-olds are doing.

Some first, second, and third graders are meeting under the trees. It is a small church so this relieves the congestion inside. At first the boys and girls draw on lapboards. Then they gather around the teacher in an informal group for conversation and a story. They sing, too, and bow their heads in prayer. Later, the children dramatize the story.

12

Oscar J. Rumpf

Vacation church school gives opportunities for outdoor activities.

Summer is the church's opportunity to serve all ages.

Oscar J. Rumpf

A group of junior highs come out of the church in the late morning and start off together. Is it a trip they are going to take or an observation tour of some kind?

Vacation? Why, yes, who could have as much fun alone? And vacations can be filled with learning opportunities. Who but consecrated Christians could have been so resourceful and wise in the ways of God for growing boys and girls? But these outside observations lead one inside the church. Curiosity is piqued. There must be something more. What spirit moves a church people to consider the summer as the church's great opportunity—so often untapped, but here so evidently employed and enjoyed?

Indoors one finds an atmosphere of relaxation and happy activity. There seems to be an outstanding combination

How inviting the easel is to young children!

Oscar J. Rumpf

Oscar J. Rumpf

Children work in an atmosphere of relaxation and happy activity.

of purposeful teaching and eager learning by doing. Groups of ten to twenty boys and girls with adult leaders and older youth assistants are spread out in different parts of the building, in the yard, and on a nearby screened porch of a large home. Each space seems to belong to the group meeting there and is set up with furniture and equipment conducive to group living and learning.

How inviting the easels and large paint brushes are to the four- and five-year-olds! All are playing at work, either in keeping house, caring for baby dolls, building a garage, watering flowers in the window box, or painting pictures to decorate the windows of this home. One notes the free, vigorous, and satisfying ways in which young children assume one role after another as they are given opportunity to play father, mother, truck driver, nurse, doctor, or even the tractor that plows a field and pulls a load of hay. Needs of children are revealed in this spontaneous play. Teachers note

15

these needs as guides to constructive learning so that through their play children learn to understand other people better and to work together helpfully as co-operating partners in group living. There are high points of awareness: appreciation lifted Godward in moments of song and prayer and concern for others finding expression in giving and serving.

Activities are of such a variety as one seldom sees in a Sunday church school. Having more space to spread out in and more time for completion, the older boys and girls can carry out activities that are not limited to desk work and sitting still. The fourth, fifth, and sixth graders may have an outdoor map as big as an ordinary garage. The "mountains . . . round about Jerusalem," the steep Jericho road, the highway where caravans passed near the boyhood home of Jesus and the fruitful plains of Esdraelon, now give visual imagery to Bible stories.

Through their play children learn to understand others.

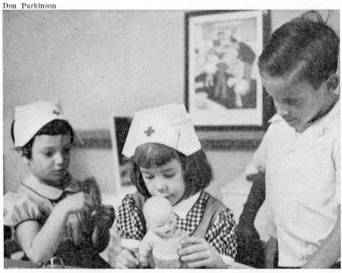

Developing reading interests are expected as children mature.

Words are easily forgotten unless they are rooted in experience.

17

The making of a tape recording and a movie with photography by a father keep the junior-high pupils working for days with the Bible, Bible dictionaries, and other background materials. It is evident from watching the various working groups that the theme of the vacation church school is the Bible. Each year there is a different theme around which to organize the work of the school so as to provide for the all-round Christian growth of boys and girls toward great continuing goals.

It is revealed in group after group that these boys and girls are growing religiously through their intimate small group relationships and their association with Christian adult leaders over a period of time. Blocks of time! Blessed time! Enough hours together to follow through on a big enough piece of work to be a challenge and to permit learning to take place. For learning does not come by the clock. It comes through achievement and fulfillment—by doing and living and evaluating and then attempting new goals.

Planning goes on all over the place—not just teacher planning but planning by boys and girls. True, the planning done by the very young is for the current day—or perhaps the tomorrow—but boys and girls in elementary grades and junior high groups make increasingly long-range plans. They plan ways of getting needed information. They plan to give some service to a worthy cause. Older ones plan their own worship services. Some plan ways of recording and sharing their discoveries. Such plans seem to involve a great deal of work to be done—research, thinking, observation tours, interviews, study, construction activities, service activities, art activities, dramatic activities, memorizing—but all such work under the guidance of purposeful teachers is the means of learning and growing in Christian living.

These boys and girls discover the value of their own plans and work as they progress toward their goals, and seek to improve their ideas, their spirit, and their work together. What churchmen they will make—learning to work hard together and then checking on the results. "Was our work

Oscar J. Rumpf

Summertime is church time as children learn and grow.

well done?" "Did we do our best?" How wonderful that these boys and girls are learning to recognize pettiness and selfishness as handicaps. Think what it will mean for the work of the Kingdom if self-appraisal and group evaluation are carried over into their work as adults. What if all church members dared to evaluate their own spirit of co-operation, sense of responsibility, and concern for others?

Opportunity for progressive experiences is essential in growth, and progress is essential in maintaining interest. Even when all of the boys and girls have left for the day, a look around at their work and recalling the day's experiences reveal progression in skills, developing reading interests, deepening of thought and spiritual awareness, growing concern for others, and greater skill in social relationships. Such progression is to be expected in careful grading and good teaching.

What is the vacation church school? It is all that we have seen plus a lot of intangible growth which is one of the mysteries of God. Does this picture seem too good to be true? Then it shall be my challenge. Does it look ideal? Then I shall put it in my long-time planning for my church. And then, God willing and blessing diligent efforts, there shall come a day when summertime is churchtime so that boys and girls may grow toward God in Christlike living of this kind.

Summary— The vacation church school is a summer week-day school of the church for boys and girls.

It is an ecumenical experience.

It is an opportunity for the church.

It is a school and a vacation with religious significance.

It is an atmosphere of relaxation and happy activity.

The vacation church school is group living and learning in a permissive atmosphere.

It is time enough for pupils to plan, achieve, and evaluate.

It is a place to meet the needs of boys and girls through a variety of experiences.

Suggestions for Things to Do

The story in this chapter is both historical and legendary. It pictures some of the best, culled from the experiences of many people, churches, and denominations. It is not an unattainable ideal, but a practical realization in many places and under many conditions, in cities, in rural areas, and in camps and in settlements.

1. Find out what the story is in your community. Begin with your own church. If there has never been a vacation church school, the story has yet to be written.

2. Make an outline of the story of the vacation church school that you would like to see in your community. A clear picture created by you may serve as a blueprint for the best possible vacation church school.

A Day in the Vacation Church School

VISITING THE KINDERGARTEN

WHAT REALLY GOES ON IN ANY ONE DAY IN A VACATION church school? To find the answer let us visit one department and stay throughout the morning's session. Not every day would be the same, of course, nor would any two departments be following the same procedures and activities, for all good schools are graded. Any department we visit, however, is just one illustration of the principles that should apply to all age groups. Today we choose to visit the kindergarten children, who are four and five years of age.

A visitor has some responsibility to make intelligent observations. We shall be better observers when we are prepared to look for principles that should apply to all good teaching at every age level. In this chapter we seek illustrations of these principles in the kindergarten as follows:

> a variety of activities
> opportunities for children to make choices, decisions, and plans
> creative but purposeful use of materials
> attention to individual needs and interests
> worship growing out of other experiences
> a carefully planned but flexible schedule
> opportunity for children to learn truths as they put them into practice
> need for evaluation by teachers as they plan for the future in terms of what has happened
> careful preparation, including room for each day
> each session a part of a larger experience and purpose

21

The Day Begins With Teachers — A day in the vacation church school begins with teachers. For them each day is an important part of a larger ongoing experience in learning. Teachers are aware that big purposes are not achieved in a day, so their purpose for one session is just a segment of larger purposes to be achieved through a number of related sessions. For example, the purpose of the unit used with kindergarten children for an entire vacation school period may be:

> to help four- and five-year-old children grow in an understanding of Jesus as a kind friend to others; and to discover ways of being kind friends, too.

The purpose for one day may be to help children discover that Jesus was friendly to a sick person. Teachers will know that Jesus was always sensitive to human need although kindergarten children are discovering just one example of it at a time. Yes, the day begins with teachers who are thinking and planning for the days ahead as well as for this present day.

The Room Teaches — The day begins for teachers in another way. They prepare the room to stimulate activity and encourage learning. Good teachers know that it is important to set up a room that invites children to work, play, sing, and worship, so a housekeeping center is set up with all the necessary equipment for sweeping, dusting, washing dishes, doing the laundry, and cooking dinner. A large place is chosen for a block center, and a rug is provided so that block building will be less disturbing. But there is plenty of room, for this is a popular place. There are bookshelves and a low reading table by the window. Painting easels stand ready to use with the paint mixed and aprons for painters to wear while at work. There are tables set up for drawing, modeling, and creative cutting and pasting. There

Don Parkinson

The block center is a popular place for group play.

is also a nature table with interesting objects to be looked at and enjoyed.

In their preparation for the day, teachers seek to appeal to all the senses—colors to see and choose, modeling materials to handle, music to hear, fruit juice to taste, and flowers to smell and see. The room is set up to invite a variety of interests and activities. But in the variety of learning materials there is order. Materials that belong together are grouped together. There are shelves and low cupboards where four- and five-year-old children can put away toys and working materials when they are through using them at the various interest centers.

Arriving Children Become Absorbed in Activities — It is still twenty minutes before the announced time of the session. Observers are in their places. Teachers are already at the work and play centers, and now the children are beginning to arrive. John and Timmy stop to play with the blocks.

23

The truck is much in evidence as a bridge is being built. When Deanne arrives, she goes straight to the housekeeping center, where she washes doll clothes in warm soapy suds in a rhythmic fashion and with complete absorption. Others choose to draw or paint or look at books. Teachers are alert to give guidance and enter into play experiences. Sometimes the teacher starts singing an appropriate song that fits into what the children are doing.

Soon the children are engaged in play of their own choosing. Mark arrives for the first time and is content to watch the children. In a little while the teacher suggests that they look at a book together. Mark is willing and is soon very interested in the story. Three or four other children join them; and still others nearby, although busy with some other activity, edge near enough to overhear what is being read.

The Values of Play — The work and play period lasts about an hour. Some kindergarten children play a long time at one center, but most of them frequently change and follow a variety of interests. Often a child gets emotional release when he can put on an apron and finger paint or model with clay or wash doll clothes. He finds real satisfaction in these activities and is helped to relax.

There is Jimmy who did not have time for his favorite breakfast game—watching the cereal soak up the milk. It is time for vacation church school, and his mother is hurrying him. In fact, Jimmy does not have time to follow up any of his interests, and he resents having to hurry, hurry, hurry. When he arrives at the church, Jimmy is still cross and resentful. But he soon finds modeling materials—clay, wallpaper cleaner, or salt and flour dough, all of which he can punch and push and pound as much as he wishes. These materials give Jimmy a chance to release hostile feelings that pile up when he is hurried and his own desires are being thwarted. After a few minutes he is relaxed.

Play offers many opportunities to be creative, too. When

24

A sense of personal worth comes through play of one's own choosing.

a child is creative, he has an increased sense of worth. Only those who think of themselves as having worth can believe that others think of them highly, too. In the kindergarten there is opportunity to be creative with blocks, paints, crayons, clay, and housekeeping equipment where children dramatize home play.

A collage is enjoyed by some young children and offers an opportunity for making creative pictures. A collage is an abstract composition using many kinds of materials—small pieces of velvet, cotton, yarn, rickrack, paper straws, buttons of all sizes, leather scraps, pipe cleaners, sequins, and so on. Do you remember how your fingers itched to get into sewing boxes containing some of these treasures? Do you recall how you loved to play with scraps of sewing pieces? Children see so much that they cannot handle, but in this activity they may choose whatever they want to make a picture on paper.

Mike sits at the table where there are paper, scissors, paste, gummed tape, and the collage. He combines wonderful colors. Mike lives in a pink colored house so he makes a house of pink rickrack pasted on the paper. He uses green paper straws for trimming and a lavender button for the door. Sandra has a real sense of design. She makes a V shape using a piece of green cloth. She adds a circle of blue, using white buttons at the top center. Then adds more circles of red, blue, silver, gold, and dark blue sequins to the design. A line at the bottom is made of red rickrack. Everyone was interested in watching Winn make a rabbit. Someone seeing it exclaimed, "Winn made a real thing!"

The Religious Values of Play— How does one reach a child where he truly lives? What is the young child's interest, his business? The child's business is play. Play is his work, and he needs it as much as he needs food and shelter. It is through play that the child learns. Through play he learns what his world is like; he learns about himself; he learns about others. Through play he experiments with life using all of his senses. It is through play that the child learns to keep himself busy, to become absorbed in what he is doing, and to give himself to his own activity. Many adults do not achieve because they have never learned to give themselves to their work, and play is a child's work.

A child finds out what life is like as he imitates the work of his elders. This he does with toys. A toy truck must be made to do things like a big truck so the child grapples with problem situations, finds solutions, and gains assurance in meeting and solving problems. Trucks are a means of doing good—of serving the needs of people. They take garden and farm produce to market; they haul coal from the mines. All these are things to be used for the welfare of humankind. This is basic learning if one is to practice the principles of Jesus.

The Christian religion is a way of living. One's relationships are especially involved: his relationship to God, his relationship to himself, and his relationships to others. Love is the keynote in these relationships, but love is an intangible quality that must find expression in tangible ways. All material possessions, such as food, money, toys, and tools, may be the means of expressing and showing concern and care for others, of expressing one's self, and of growing in a sense of personal worth. These are some of the qualities of a true child of God, and basic to this conception one needs to learn to use the physical and material to serve spiritual ends. It is the business of the church to help children with this learning.

Through play experiences where children have to share, take turns, and respect the rights of others, the Golden Rule comes alive. This work and play period in the kindergarten is one of the most rewarding periods of the day where children begin to practice the Christian way of social behavior as a part of their daily living.

Group Living and Learning Continues — Teachers watch for interest lags, helping children who do not know how to

27

keep themselves busy to find new activities. In the schedule there comes a time to clean up the room, but no child is stopped immediately. A warning signal is given so that he does not have to stop his work abruptly. Paintbrushes are washed; the dishwater is emptied; doll clothes are hung up to dry; blocks are piled on the shelf; books are put away. Everything is in its place. Then comes the time when a few children go with an assistant to the toilet and wash their hands. While this is being done, the leading teacher starts playing a finger play or simple game until everyone is ready for lunch.

Children are chosen to pass napkins and pour juice from small pitchers. Everyone waits to be served, and then a simple thank-you prayer is said, "We are glad, dear God, for fresh orange juice that helps us grow strong." Informal conversation is carried on. This informal fellowship time of drinking juice and talking lasts from ten to fifteen minutes. Following this comes a rest period on individual mats. The children settle down as the teacher sings softly or tells a story or plays soft music on the piano or record player. After a ten- to fifteen-minute rest, the teacher gives a wake-up signal. The children fold up their mats and put them away according to directions. Then they gather around the teacher in an informal group to talk over the happy times at vacation church school.

"What did you like best of all this morning?" asks the teacher. "Washing dishes," responds Mike. "Playing train," says Jimmy. And so the children respond. The teacher finally summarizes by saying, "When we work and play together, we are friends." The children then sing, "Friends! Friends! Friends!" and "A Happy Day." "We are friends when we help one another," says the teacher. "There is a verse in the Bible about it." With the open Bible in her hand, she reads, "A friend is friendly at all times." "Jesus was friendly, too, to people who needed him. There is a story in our Bible about his helping Simon's mother-in-law when she was sick." After the story the teacher bows her head and prays: "Thank you, God, that Jesus knew how to help people. Help us to learn

28

how to be helpers, too." Then the children sing "Jesus Went About Doing Good."

"There are many ways children can be helpful and make people happy," says the teacher. Then she sings a story-song about Timmy who does so many things to help. "He brings slippers for his daddy. He picks up baby sister's toys and shuts the door for Grandmother without making any noise. Timmy goes about doing good."

"We can help, too," say the children as they begin to name things they can do. The last few moments are spent playing a game, "This is the way we help at home because we're growing bigger." Each child shows something he can do, and the rest guess by his actions how he is helping at home. All the children who wish have a turn and the play continues as long as there is interest.

"We can make a big story about helping," suggests the teacher, as she shows a strip of paper and pictures of children helping. Across the top of the paper is printed "Stories of Helpers." "Any who wish may work on this tomorrow when you come," she says. Then it is time to go home. It is evident by the way the children say good-by that they have had a good time. And now only the teachers are left.

It was evident to the observers from the very first that the purpose of work in this session was to help children "do good" and "show friendliness."

The Day Ends With Teachers — And so the day at vacation church school begins and ends with teachers. Now they talk together about the morning session. The leading teacher asked, "How is Sue growing in her ability to play with other children? How can we find out about Buddy's tension? What can be done about it in the kindergarten?" As these problems are discussed, plans are made for the next day. Each teacher assumes some of the special duties. It has been a good day. Each has been a working partner with God in guiding the Christian growth of these young children.

29

What Did This Day Do for Children? — It is to be noted first of all that the day has a flexible schedule. The needs of the children, their interest span, the materials of the lesson unit, the day's activities, and the children's work and play relationships all help determine the schedule. On this particular day the schedule was somewhat as follows:

APPROXIMATE TIME	ACTIVITY
50-60 minutes	Play at interest centers
15 minutes	Clean up room, toilet, wash hands
10-12 minutes	Lunch and informal fellowship
10-15 minutes	Rest period
40 minutes	Conversation, evaluate w o r k, sing, story, worship moments, games, plan for a poster

Some of the results to a young child spending such a day in the vacation church school are:

In the play period the child learns to keep himself busy and to find interesting things to do. He experiences the give and take of group life, the need for sharing, and the satisfaction that comes from it. He learns how to take turns and respect the rights of others. What the play at the interest centers means to any one child depends upon his needs. If a child seems afraid of making contacts with others, seems tense or uneasy, having opportunities to use a variety of materials in a vacation church school helps him become more friendly, relaxed, and sociable.

Persons who have studied children and their play say that clay offers a medium both for destruction without guilt and for construction with satisfaction. Blocks provide a means of adventure which is safe. Children have the urge to run the risks and experience the dangers which they see adults experience. With blocks a child may imitate many dangerous situations and prove his ability to handle these situations. Blocks can become an environment which a child can control so that he does not always feel dominated, or at the mercy of the environment in which he lives.

When children are thwarted in their purposes and when they are under pressure to conform to adult pleasures and standards, they may become tense, resentful, aggressive, or negative. Fortunately, children are able to accept some alternates for activities that are denied them. If these substitute activities allow the children to release tension and hostile feelings, it may prevent them from behaving in undesirable ways. It is necessary for children to get rid of such feelings lest they be driven into the unconscious to continue their damage.

The therapeutic value of play is also seen in water play as it becomes a substitute for many activities denied children in real life, such as forbidden play with water and dirt, the constant nagging to keep clean, or the fear of

Opportunities to use a variety of materials help children become relaxed.

Don Parkinson

31

punishment if they do not do so. Good teachers try to understand children's play and seek to make it possible for each child to be released to be his best self and achieve his highest potential. For further help on this topic read *Understanding Children's Play* by R. E. Hartley, *et al.* (see Bibliography).

In the vacation church school kindergarten a child hears a few stories from the Bible for which he is ready. In the situation described in this chapter the child learned that Jesus was a helpful friend and experienced what it means to be helpful, himself. All the child's experiences of the day offered opportunity for practicing friendliness and for coming to the realization that this is a good way to live.

A Follow-up Report — To show that each day is not the same and that any one day is a part of the whole vacation church school experience, the teacher sent the observers this note:

"I thought you might be interested in the conclusion of our unit. We planned a visit to Mrs. Howard, a shut-in who lived about four blocks from the church. The children and I planned how we would walk and how we would talk and what we would do. The children suggested that we sing 'Jesus Went About Doing Good,' which we did. The shut-in told us how she used to teach Sunday school and that she liked to hear children sing. Two large bouquets of flowers had been brought to give to Mrs. Howard. Pictures of Jesus made into a book and tied in a painted paper folder that one of the children made with finger paint were also given. When Mrs. Howard looked at the picture in the book, she said, 'I will keep this always.'

"When we returned to the church, the teachers had planned that the children would want their juice and crackers. However, the walk was so long and it was so warm the children were tired. The first boy in the room threw himself on his mat. Each child did the same so one of the teachers went to the piano and played a lullaby.

"We had previously planned that the children would evaluate the trip in a group, but seeing them so relaxed, I said, 'Let us talk about our trip while we are stretched out on our mats. How do you know Mrs. Howard was happy because we came?' Some of the answers were: 'She liked our flowers.' 'She liked the book about Jesus and said she would always keep it.' 'She smiled when we sang.' 'I think she was happy because we took time to go see her.' Then I prayed, 'Thank you, God, for Jesus, who went about doing good. Thank you that Mrs. Howard let us come to see her and that she liked the flowers and the book. We are glad that we did take time to go and see her.'

"We talked awhile about older people who lived near us and ways of making them happy. Then when rest was over, we went to the tables for juice."

Summary — The day begins with teachers.

Plans are made in terms of specific purposes to be achieved.

The room is prepared to stimulate activity and learning.

Arriving children become absorbed in activities, choosing from among a variety of experiences.

Play is therapeutic, providing emotional release, an opportunity to be creative, and a developing sense of worth.

Boys and girls learn through what they practice.

Evaluating the day is important in order to plan tomorrow.

The day's activities and the children's work and play relationships all help determine the day's schedule.

There are religious reasons for play.

Suggestions for Things to Do

1. How significant are the opportunities for activity in your department room?

2. List the work and play areas in one column, and in a parallel column list the possible play activities your equipment allows. Then with a different color pencil, add what you would like to include in both columns.

In the Vacation Church School

WITH JUNIOR BOYS AND GIRLS

"I WOULD NOT KNOW WHAT TO DO WITH SO MUCH TIME," WAS the reply of one prospective teacher when her pastor enlisted her help in the vacation church school. She had taught only in short sessions of thirty and forty minutes. After three weeks in a vacation church school the same teacher's comment was, "We all wished for at least another week." How the time was used during the three weeks and how the work developed in the group is revealed in the following story as told by the teachers of a class for fourth, fifth, and sixth graders in a village vacation church school:

The first session was on Wednesday with ten boys and girls present. It was the second week after public school closed. Unfortunately, there had been no co-operative planning with other agencies of the town; consequently there was much competition for the time of the boys and girls, and our enrollment was small. The Girl Scouts were having a day camp. The town park was opening a Monday-Wednesday-Friday morning swim period for nine- to eleven-year-old boys. By the next Monday, however, there were nineteen junior pupils attending vacation church school.

The textbook, *Finding God Through Work and Worship*, by McWhirter was studied about six weeks in advance of the opening of the school. The teachers met once a week to plan together, and we studied individually between times. We kept comparing the purposes stated in the textbook with what we knew about the needs of our boys and girls and our local conditions. We came out with a fairly clear idea of what we wanted to have happen

34

to our boys and girls this summer. At first we wondered how we could get an "action or experience approach" (a new phrase we learned at the county vacation church school institute). We finally decided that in our case it meant that the boys and girls would learn to find God through worship only if they really wanted to and if they did something about it. What they would do was not entirely up to us, for we had to let the boys and girls have a part in the planning. We thought that we could be ready for the planning period in three ways: (1) by having some ideas of our own, (2) by creating a stimulating environment, (3) by being prepared with the tools and materials, that might be needed.

We set a day to go calling on all the boys and girls who had registered in advance and a few others who had not. We enlisted two mothers to help us with this and prepared them by stating that the purpose of our visits were:

1. To welcome the boys and girls and help them and their families feel that the church was anticipating their presence in the vacation church school.

2. To tell about the plans and purposes of the school.

In our interpretation of the program we included each of the three words: vacation, church, and school. No one would be interested in just going to school again. And it was not enough just to think of it as church. But neither was it to be just a vacation in the ordinary sense of that word. The uniqueness of the vacation church school is that it includes all three in a combination when its program is planned as an integral part of the year-round activities of the church.

Getting the Room Ready — We teachers went together to prepare the room on Monday before our school started on Wednesday. We took down pictures, cleared shelves, and fairly stripped the room of everything left from any former use that had been made of it. We wanted to start a new experience there, and we wanted the room to help us get

35

into that new experience, namely, to help us find God through worship. The supplies and working tools were arranged so that the boys and girls would know where these things belonged, where to get them, and where to put them away. The following pictures were put up on the eye level of the boys and girls:

"The Hilltop at Nazareth" by Wood

"The Angelus" by Millet

Other pictures showed:

a family saying grace at table

people worshiping at church

a family reading the Bible

two juniors preparing a worship center

a junior choir

a boy sitting on a hilltop, looking thoughtful

By each picture was an envelope containing several blank slips of paper.

There was a browsing table near the windows with such books as One God—The Ways We Worship Him by Fitch (Lothrop, Lee and Shepard), Thoughts of God for Boys and Girls by Welker and Barber (Harper and Brothers), denominational devotional booklets, a church hymnal, a junior hymnal, worship services from denominational magazines which seemed to us to have value for use in our unit. These worship services were mounted on construction paper with room to add a picture. A box of small pictures was ready for this purpose.

The First Day — As the pupils arrived, they found teachers trying to think of names appropriate for the pictures that were on the walls. As each pupil made a choice, he cast his vote for a name in the envelopes beside the pictures. We asked the arriving boys and girls to join us, saying the group could select later the name they thought best. The first ones, already at work putting names in the envelopes, enlisted the participation of the late arrivals. By the time all were finished, one teacher and four boys and

36

Jerome Drown

Vacation church school gives time to study church windows.

girls were finding and mounting pictures on the worship service cards.

Since the boys and girls did not all come from the same church, nor from the same public school, we had combined a playtime and get-acquainted time out under the trees. Just before returning to the room, we suggested a detour to the church sanctuary, beginning a "line of silence" from the church door until we reached our classroom again.

The reason given for going to the sanctuary was to look

37

at it for any ways in which it helped people find and worship God. It was also suggested that we each spend a moment in silent worship before we left. Another teacher had preceded us and was standing near the front of the chapel looking up at a stained glass window. This seemed to suggest, or reinforce the suggestion, that we look around. When the teacher bowed her head, others soon followed, and then she sang "The Lord is in his holy temple; let all the earth keep silence before him." After a brief moment we returned to our classroom where the juniors formed into committees to select from the envelopes the best name for each picture.

Planning Our Work — We began this planning period with the boys and girls with a feeling that our unit was already introduced, so the leader said, "People do many different kinds of things at church, but one of the most important reasons for a church is to help people find God and worship him. Our vacation church school can do that for us, but even though that is what we work on, there are many ways of doing it. You will, therefore, want to make some choices about the work we shall do together. You may have some suggestions about ways in which to find out about God through worship. Miss Laird and I have some ideas, too. Let us use this chart for our ideas. It is entitled 'Vacation church school plans that will help us learn about God through worship.' "

As suggestions were given by the boys and girls and teachers, the items were listed on the chart:

> Learn to sing hymns
> Plan a worship service
> Make a worship center in our room
> Spatter print a hanging and a table cover to
>   match
> Make a report
> Make a bookmark for the Bible

Be a verse-reading choir
Create a litany
Visit Mrs. Brown, a shut-in, and have a worship
service. (This came in response to the leader's
question, "Are there people who do not get
to worship services who might enjoy one?")

Space was left on the chart so that we might add other
suggestions as we thought of them.

The boys and girls were selected to make a hanging and
matching table cover, and suggestions were made for beginning the work. The table top and wall spaces were
measured. A committee volunteered to find and purchase
the material for the hanging and table cover. Others were
to look for and press long grasses and sprays of leaves for
use in making the spatter print design.

Teachers Evaluate the First Session — In the evaluation the
teachers thought about the first day's motivation and whether
it was strong enough to create an anticipation for the days
ahead. Did the boys and girls have any chance to determine
what they would like to do? We decided that perhaps we
had overweighted the situation so that it would go the way
we wanted it. As far as the teachers could tell, all the group
had entered into and seemingly anticipated the making
of the spatter print except Danny Marlowe, who was quiet
and evidently not enthusiastic. We didn't know Danny
too well, except that he was a woodworking enthusiast and
spent a great deal of time in his father's basement work-
shop. That gave us an idea, and Miss Laird made a telephone call there that night. The next day another item
was added on the chart to our list of things to do: Make an
Offering Bowl.

Boys and Girls Have Work to Do— Working on spatter
prints and leaf prints kept several children busy. Danny
whittled away on his wooden offering bowl. Imagining

39

Boys and girls learn about God's world through activities.

ahead what it would be like to use the spatter prints, someone suggested that they be initiated in a worship service. Much time was spent selecting a worship theme, Scripture, prayers, and hymns.

It began to be rumored that our attendance would be increased in the coming week. The day camp would be over, and some of the other boys and girls who had not previously enrolled were getting interested. Part of Friday was spent in planning ways in which the newcomers could be helped to catch up with those who had the three-day start. When faced with the question, the group decided that the new ones should start the way they did, by naming pictures. This meant going through the files and finding new pictures which were appropriate, for, as the boys and girls said, "We have already named these." Another request was that the incoming group have a chance to go to the sanctuary, and plans were made by the boys and girls for that activity. Several volunteered to come early enough to meet and register the new pupils and to help them get started.

On Monday the teachers were surprised both at how quickly the nine new pupils seemed to catch on and the pride with which last week's group explained their work. It was soon evident that more work needed to be planned. There were now more hands than were needed to finish the spatter prints and leaf prints, so the whole group met together for another planning period.

Because music plays so large a part in worship, the juniors were interested to find out more about the place and use of music. We realized that music was associated with worship even in Bible times. The teachers had secured from the library a book including the making of shepherds' pipes. The teachers had also secured some green willow twigs and had these displayed as a separate interest center. Tools for working on this project were also on the table.

By coincidence, some of the children attending day camp had made shepherds' pipes the week before. The whole discussion about such musical instruments was an incentive for introducing Psalms 150, with the unexpected outcome that almost all the children began volunteering to bring whatever they had with which "to make praise." Real musicians might have called the outcome noise, but enthusiasm soared. At least everyone could unite on simple chants with flutaphones, recorders, bamboo pipes, musical combs, and all the rest.

New plans were decided on and added to the list on the chart as follows:

> Have spatter prints and worship center ready for Thursday
> Learn to chant more Bible verses
> Finish learning Psalms 150 as a verse-reading choir;
> Chant a praise verse while using instruments
> Make worship centers to use at home
> Copy prayers (or make them up) to use at home.

41

Because the pupils suggested that we invite people to our worship service "to show how well we can do," the leader told Jesus' story of the two men who went up to the Temple to pray—one a proud Pharisee and the other a humble publican. Volunteers to dramatize the parts of this story were immediate. First, there was Marilyn as the Pharisee—Marilyn, who was prone to announce, "My father is a professor so I know," or, "I think we ought to do it this way," or, "I'm sure I could do that real well." Vivian, a Negro girl, was the publican. She resented Marilyn's dominance, and in dramatizing the publican's part, she fell on her face to pray and prayed for mercy and forgiveness with unusual fervor, but included "Help me not to be like this proud Pharisee." Somehow no child called attention to this slip, but the teachers recognized the need of the two girls to find both a deeper relationship to God and an understanding and appreciation of themselves and each other. "To show how well we can do" was not suggested again.

Materials, Activities, and Understandings — While boys and girls plan in terms of action and things to do, the leader introduces them to materials which are needed in carrying out their plans, and which enrich and interpret the work they are doing. Sometimes this enrichment material itself stimulates new or further activity. When the picture, "The Angelus," was studied for use in the worship center, someone suggested making this a living picture by posing it. There was quite a discussion in the committee as the participants had smeared themselves with dirt, explaining that the people in the picture must have been dirty after digging potatoes all day. But others answered reasonably, "You don't want to make people laugh. You want to make them worship God."

And along with related materials and activities there were discoveries about the boys and girls themselves, not just by the teachers, but by the boys and girls themselves.

The picture posing got off to a bad start because some boys and girls giggled. Then it was tried again with "Do you think you can keep yourselves steady?"

It was a revealing day when boys and girls portrayed in charade form some ways they would like to grow through worship. "Since one should live better as a result of worship, in what ways would you like to grow?" asked the teacher. The answers were to be acted out in charades by teams working together. Some personal goals were set up in this way. As each pupil set up a goal for himself, he wrote it out and took it home for his worship center so that he might continue to make it a matter of prayer.

A picnic was planned as another way to draw closer to one another, to know God better, and to continue the group's interests. After very active play we listened to a story about a lad who spent a day fishing and who learned while alone in the outdoors that God is very near at all times. Several of the musical instruments had been brought to the picnic. The boys and girls spent some time trying to work out the notes of the chants on the melody bells (bells on one octave), recorders, and shepherds' pipes. The day before, the group had composed their own tune for chanting Psalms 47:6-7.

A watermelon treat was enjoyed at the picnic. The picnic closed with a prayer circle that seemed to fit into the feelings and desires as naturally as the watermelon feed.

Worship Services and Evaluations — The first worship service the juniors prepared was something of a disappointment. It would have left us very depressed if we had not recognized it as a learning opportunity and given the pupils a chance to evaluate it later in the morning. As soon as the leader asked, "How well did we do in leading our worship service this morning?" several answered at once, "We didn't know it well enough." Then came suggestions for improving it another time: "We should practice it more"; "We need to practice the words"; "We should find our places in the

43

Bible beforehand"; "We didn't always know what we were supposed to do."

When the second worship service was evaluated, one pupil said, "We really learned we had to get it ready. I thought it was better because we used our own prayer instead of reading one out of a book." And this was their own prayer:

> Our Father God, we thank you for this beautiful world; for land and water; for rivers and for people; for friends and family. God, who has made all so beautiful, we thank you for making the earth and for making us. Forgive us for all the naughty things we have done. Help us to be better persons, to do our work willingly, and to care for our brothers and sisters without being told. May we have beautiful thoughts inside us and help spread your love all around. Amen.

About this time we began planning to conclude our work. As is often the case, the boys and girls wanted to invite their parents. For the benefit of the parents they wanted to get in some of everything accomplished in the three weeks. For instance, when planning the worship service the boys and girls chose the worship materials we had used before. They also wanted to give a play. This meant giving up outdoor play to prepare and polish some of those role-playing scenes they had done. But everyone seemed convinced that preparation and practice were necessary.

One of the teachers had told the boys and girls that the next week she was going to a vacation church school that was to be conducted in another part of the county for migrant children. Offerings had been made in the worship services so that supplies might be bought for this vacation school. Mary Donna was chosen to explain it to the parents. She made quite an appeal and then turned teacherlike by saying, "Put up your hands if you think we ought to give a lot." The offering moved up to nine dollars, and then the boys and girls made another gift, a presentation of the spatter print hanging and table cover. Such generosity caused Roberta to squirm as she whispered, "I'd sure like to keep it myself." Roberta did not have many pretty things at home.

Teachers Evaluate — We thought everything would be over at 11:30 on that last morning. We were busy bidding parents and children good-by, but there seemed to be a circle of boys and girls around the door and no one was leaving. Soon two of them came back asking, "Why can't we all go to the chapel with our mothers before we leave?" Of course we went. According to our custom, we stood quietly and then sang, "The Lord Is in His Holy Temple." How did the mothers and little brothers and sisters know to be quiet? Two pupils stood at the door with fingers on their lips.

We teachers went back to the classroom after all had gone. We wondered why we had not thought of that climactic touch. Then we discovered that to some extent, at least, we had achieved an "action or experience approach," that the school was no longer just ours. Somewhere along the way it had become the vacation church school for junior boys and girls. Neither of us had ever taught in permissive atmosphere like that of our vacation church school. Now we knew what an "action or experience approach" meant and to say "time permits." Two and a half hours a day for three weeks gave enough time for changes to take place. It gave time for teachers to learn to know boys and girls better. It gave time for boys and girls to come to some new understandings of themselves and one another as they worked and played together in a relaxed group experience of planning, doing, and evaluating. Yes, time and activity are needed for growth—spiritual as well as physical—and growth seems to be God's favorite way of achieving change.

Summary — Teachers plan in advance by comparing purposes in the textbooks with the needs of their boys and girls.

There is home visitation to welcome children and to inform parents and boys and girls of plans and purposes of the school.

The room is prepared in advance, and the first day involves pupil participation in work to be done, in getting acquainted, and in planning ahead.

Teachers evaluate the pupil's interests, their involvement, and their leadership as members of a group.

Boys and girls have important work to do as they decide on plans and carry them out. This includes initiating the newcomers into the group. This means improving relationships with one another.

Leaders provide a variety of enrichment materials and activities in terms of things to do to stimulate new interests and to guide pupils in understanding themselves and evaluate what they do.

The work is fittingly concluded and evaluated by every teacher in the vacation church school in terms of how the children have grown.

Suggestions for Things to Do

1. Examine your denominational and the co-operative series of vacation church school textbooks. Study them carefully in the light of the following:

a) In terms of their purposes which course would best meet the needs of your own junior boys and girls at this particular time?

b) In terms of activities suggested, through which activities would the talents and potential abilities of your group find the greatest expression?

Analyze two of the larger activities to see what talents and abilities would be developed. What new skills would teachers need to learn in order to lead pupils in these activities?

2. Make a list of the essential characteristics of a group of boys and girls that participates in planning, doing, and evaluating their own work and conduct.

4

Special Events

IN THE VACATION CHURCH SCHOOL PROGRAM

MUCH OF LIFE IS LIVED ON A ROUTINE LEVEL. WE RECOGNIZE that work gets done in a planned day-by-day schedule; thus achievements are won, and life accomplishes much of its mission. All people who achieve know what is meant by the "daily grind." Jesus spent many of his days teaching, healing, and laboring to lead people to understand and practice the way of God.

Jesus knew what it meant to labor consistently and until he was weary. But there were high moments and times of refreshment. There was a mountaintop experience, too. It was good, but Jesus was not tempted to stay there. He went back to the valley to his work. Jesus also made it a practice to attend some of the religious festivals of his people. But even when Jesus went to one such festival at the age of twelve, it became an occasion for discovering the deeper meanings of being about his Father's business. With Jesus the high moments always seemed related to his daily work and lifetime mission to be of service to others.

This same pattern of living may well be applied to the vacation church school and affects the way in which we look at special events. The day-by-day work results in real learning and growing; it is the accepted and usual characteristic of the vacation church school. This daily work needs to be kept uncluttered from distractions. The vacation church school is not an extended picnic for boys and girls. It is not a time in which to get ready for a closing program. The ongoing work of each department is the vacation church school, and yet there are some special events.

New Insights Into the Meaning of Special Events — There was a time when we thought that a special event must break into the ongoing program, setting it aside for the time being. Or, a special event entirely unrelated was held some evening or afternoon when the regular day was over. At such times regular grading and grouping of the boys and girls were completely ignored. The larger the crowd, either as participants or audience, the more special and successful the occasion seemed.

It is now thought that a special event is most successful when it most serves the needs of boys and girls and when it contributes most to the ongoing program and purposes. An occasion is considered special when it invigorates and renews a zest for Christian living, when it offers adventure and satisfaction, or when it celebrates a deeper awareness of and oneness with God and his other children. Such special events vary widely, according to varying situations and the needs and interests of the age groups involved.

Special Events for Different Age Groups — The first- and second- and third-grade children feel ever so much more at home in the church since they have been engaged in learning about working in the church. During the vacation church school they have collected a bulletin board of pictures of friendly people at church. Their own drawings, which they proudly display, show ways in which children may work at church. This was all part of the day-by-day work, and yet it was a very special time when their own drawings were all put on a frieze entitled, "Ways We Help at Church." Later the children gathered in front of the frieze and expressed in worship their desire to be a part of the church fellowship that represents the love and goodness of God.

Or, take the visit of Miss Reed who was in town for the summer. Miss Reed taught public-school music in the city and led a children's choir. Since Miss Reed was at home this summer, she was invited by the vacation church school director to work with the teachers, helping them with some of the music. The primary teacher told the children about Miss Reed and suggested that they invite her to teach them a new song because she knew music very well and was a friend of children. The boys and girls wrote an invitation and mailed it. They planned ways to be friendly to Miss Reed "Maybe she would like to play our game"; "We could show her our puppet play"; "We could give her some flowers"; "We could go to meet her"; "We could all try real hard to learn the song."

A corsage was made—it was a bit heavy, but Miss Reed was understanding. A committee made the room look especially nice. Two children were chosen to meet Miss Reed when she drove up in her car; another child presented the corsage. Miss Reed graciously accepted all the courtesies and taught the new song. She gained eighteen new friends. The primary boys and girls continue to look back on her visit as a very special time.

Another special event occurred when the group was invited to be guests of fourth, fifth, and sixth graders. This time the invitation was taken to the primary children, who gladly accepted it, discussed how guests express their appreciation, and made their plans on how to be guests. The juniors met the group in the hall, seated them in front-row seats, and gave some original plays on the home life in Jesus' time. Dried raisins were the only refreshment and were given out as a part of a play. To the primary children (and even more to the juniors) this visit was a special event in the vacation church school. It was interesting to note that the occasion seemed more special to the group that did the serving and made the occasion possible.

A displaced family was being brought by the church to this community, and church groups were helping furnish the house, as well as buying school clothes for the children. All were to be ready before the family's arrival. The primary boys and girls gave money and went to the store to purchase an electric clock. This was a very special day for the children. They even took the clock to the house and hung it on the kitchen wall. It was there that they stood to thank God that they could be friends to this new family coming to their community.

These few illustrations of special events for the primary and junior boys and girls would seem rather ordinary to older pupils. It is something to remember that there is a diminishing difference between an ordinary and a special event as we go down the scale in age. If a little thing can seem so special to a young child, how overwhelmed he must be by some of our events planned with older people in mind! To a young child it is largely the attitude that makes a thing special. A mother is seen preparing a sandwich and putting it in a paper bag for her five-year-old Jerry going on a picnic. Who are going? Just Jerry. How far is he going and to what place? Oh, not far, just out in the backyard. But Jerry's eyes shine, for this is a picnic!

For the older boys and girls, those of junior-high age for instance, the situation was different. Their trip to the Goodwill Industries took a two-hour ride away from home, a tour and lunch at the Institution, and a trip back later in the day. This tour was a more mature experience, but like the special occasions for the primary children it, too, contributed to ongoing purposes. While at the Goodwill Industries, the boys and girls were able to find and buy a chair for the home of the displaced family. But the group asked to have it delivered by the Goodwill's pick-up men. It was not important to the group to deliver the chair themselves. The money for the chair had been received in the offering in a worship service as planned by the junior-high boys and girls. They had studied about the Goodwill Industries—how they started, the purpose they serve, and the ways in which they are supported. The boys and girls considered their offering and the buying of the chair as support of the Goodwill Industries, and at the same

A sharing occasion that involves the whole self is most special. ▶

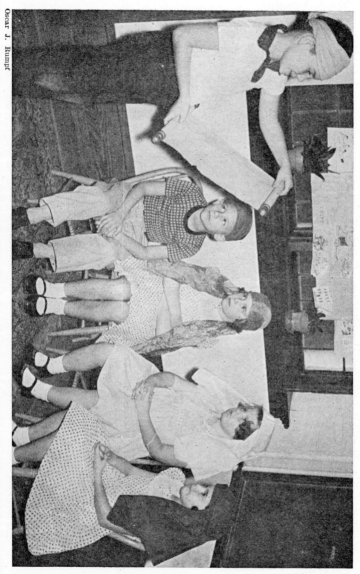

time it would be a way of helping the displaced family. In the worship service the group consecrated their efforts and the fruits of their work to God, with whom they were co-workers in the service of others.

The junior-high group was making a real survey of the community to see in what projects the churches were co-operating for the improvement of the community. They set aside part of a session to see a film of the community-chest agencies at work, and another time they saw a film on interracial relations. Seeing films was something out of the ordinary routine for these older boys and girls, but they did not consider them special events. Perhaps the evening they gave a talent show and led an evening worship service at the home for the aged stood out for them as the most special occasion of the vacation church school, even more so than a picnic held on the last day.

Programs and Ways of Bringing Work to a Close — Since a church fellowship should resemble the kind of family life in which all members are interested in what each one is doing, a vacation church school may well consider some way of sharing. This may come during or at the close of any unit of work engaged in by any one group. If the group goes about its work in normal ways, is not under pressure to prepare a special program, and is approaching the conclusion of a piece of work, it is natural for the boys and girls to share with parents and friends what to them is important and significant.

There may be a sharing time for all age groups in their own departments. It should be possible for boys and girls and their teachers to decide ways in which to reach out beyond themselves and their own group. Let them decide with whom to share and the nature of what they do. Groups can find many different ways of growing socially, of serving, and of sharing. Wise teachers may use such occasions to help the boys and girls evaluate their own work and see the importance and worth in their church-school work.

A closing program at the close of the vacation church school may be a means of dramatizing group achievement. It is a celebration of what has been completed, and it looks ahead to greater purposes. Daily life needs many such occasions to dramatize attainment and progress along the way, to spur one on to still greater heights. In fact, each unit of work should be concluded, summarized, or *highlighted* in some way, whether in a program shared with others or confined to the class group. Sometimes this is done in a worship service. Sometimes it is expressed in service that meets another's need. Sometimes it is the completing or using of something beautiful that has been created by the boys and girls themselves.

Certain cautions need to be observed when several groups join in a program. Its values may be limited because of too wide an age span and because of too many age groups to allow all of the children to share as fully as they should. Younger children, especially, need protection against the excitement of crowds and having to sit through a program that has no special meaning for them. All-school assemblies have been discontinued because of these difficulties. It is for these reasons that most group sharing is done in departments. A feeling of belonging to the larger group can be achieved in other ways, such as a visit to or from another group.

Some churches make it possible for boys and girls to share their learnings or things made with others. In one church the minister asked the junior-high boys and girls who had prepared a choral reading to give it for the Scripture lesson in the church service. The primary children, who had prepared a story about a missionary family, were asked to give it at a meeting of the Woman's Society. The juniors, who had selected slides to interpret a nature Psalm, were asked to show these slides as they read the Psalm for an adult Sunday-school class.

The director of the vacation church school, the departmental superintendents in the Sunday school, and the minister may be alerted to find ways of using what boys and girls can contribute to the general church program. It should be noted, however, that such use usually has nothing to do with the original purpose and effort. Groups have their own purposes for what they do, and this sharing is something extra, not to be overdone or to be made the important part of the whole experience.

Picnics and Other Outdoor Events — Picnics, swims, nature hikes, and other recreational features may play a very wholesome part in a vacation church school. They are usually more successful when the age range is limited to the group that regularly meets together. Recall the junior picnic described in Chapter III as an illustration of how a picnic can contribute to and continue the living of the group.

Getting overtired and overexcited are not religious experiences. They can be avoided with young children by having short picnics nearby in the churchyard, or in a neighbor's yard, or in a park. The attendance should be limited to those who regularly meet together. Sometimes mothers are included. This kind of picnic may be more frequent for it is held nearby and the refreshments are simple and are given long enough before the next meal so that appetites are not dulled. For any all-school or church family picnic it is especially necessary to consider the needs and limitations of young children. Special play provisions should be made that include understanding leadership, separate play space for various ages, and play that includes restful activities.

The family picnic sometimes involves the whole church school. Parents and staff find this a good way to get acquainted and to extend the fellowship of the church to those who are not members, or who are not in the rest of the church's program. The fellowship purposes of such an occasion should be fully realized by making everyone feel wanted and at home. Plan so that the needs and interests of all ages will be considered and so that all will receive value.

What About Movies as Special Events? — When the work of the whole school is organized around some one theme, there may be some audio-visual material of interest and value to more than one group. On the other hand, the fact that a film may be used with one group is no reason for all other groups to leave their plans and their own work to see it, too. It is necessary, then, to consider what kinds of occasions would bring groups together. The older kindergarten and the primary children may see a nature film or a Bible-story film together when similar themes are studied and each group has been prepared separately to look at it. Primary, junior, and junior-high boys and girls may have that rare occasion when the same film on Palestine, or some other common interest subject, would be of value to all. This might be true when the three groups are studying the current missionary theme. But each group will need its own preparation and its own follow-up.

A busy, active vacation church school group is not likely to feel the need for entertainment. For this reason leaders have found little purpose in showing an entertainment movie that takes up precious time and does not contribute to the ongoing work of the group. (See Chapter 9 for further use of audio-visuals.)

Summary — Life is a day-by-day achievement relieved by occasional high moments and a few mountaintop experiences.

The vacation church school is best characterized by ongoing day-by-day work and a few special events.

A special event may be good when it serves the needs of boys and girls, contributes most to ongoing purposes, invigorates and renews a zest for Christian living, introduces some new elements, and involves the whole self.

Kinds of special occasions are change and variety in the regular program, opportunities to be truly creative that yield awareness and self-realization, real worship that is a sense of oneness with God, a climactic conclusion that lifts up or dramatizes achievement, and times for fellowship and sharing with others.

Special events of sharing may differ for different age groups, such as the first, second, and third graders may make a frieze, entertain a guest, visit the juniors, buy a clock to give away.

Older boys and girls need some out-of-the-ordinary experiences on a more mature level.

All need to plan ways of bringing work to a close and to share with others.

Suggestions for Things to Do

1. Select a unit of study from the vacation church school materials suggested for the age group you teach. Make a list of the activities that might lead to a special occasion for the boys and girls. Then check each special event for:

> effectiveness in achieving the purposes of the unit
> wholehearted interest of boys and girls
> appropriateness to age level
> incentive for pupil planning and evaluation
> use of time and leading-on values
> growth in appreciation, understanding, information
> religious values and growth

2. Make plans for each age group of your vacation church school to share with parents and friends but without the typical closing program.

PART II

THE VACATION CHURCH SCHOOL BELONGS

5

The Vacation Church School Belongs

TO THE CHURCH

THE FIRST FOUR CHAPTERS OF THIS BOOK HAVE PICTURED what may happen in the vacation church school. But underneath all of the illustrations is a purpose. Each educational agency has its philosophy of education. The philosophy of Christian education is based on the religious needs of boys and girls and what our Christian faith has to offer in meeting those needs. This chapter will remind us that most needs of boys and girls are somewhat similar whether they are in church school on Sunday or in vacation church school on weekdays.

The needs which religion seeks to meet are deep and persistent, not something that can be quickly cleared up in any one hour a week even though that hour comes on Sunday morning. For this reason the church that seeks to minister to the needs of boys and girls will seek to do so in its total program. It is for this reason and in this way that the vacation church school belongs to the church.

What It Means to Belong— Let us examine the meaning of belonging. When ten-year-old Chuck says that he belongs to the Butler family, he is making a good many basic assumptions. He is assuming that there is a group who cares about him. They show love for him and concern for him. This gives Chuck a sense of security. By belonging to a family unit Chuck is not alone in the world, for the family provides comradeship in living and working relationships. There is financial support, or rather, financial co-operation, for when all of his relationships with the family

58

are two-way, they become more permanent and satisfying. Chuck contributes to his family in many ways as well as receives from them. This is one of the values of family life and gives one a sense of personal worth and a respect for the worth of others.

There is a sense in which we may think of the vacation church school as a child of the church. If each year the question is raised as to whether there is to be a vacation church school, then it has not been taken into the church family. We know that the vacation church school has been taken into the church family when the church schedules adequate time for the vacation church school, when it is written into the church budget, when its leaders are enlisted the same as for Sunday, and when the program for the summer is built on the same educational philosophy as other activities.

Unfortunately, there are many orphan vacation church schools. When the minister, Mr. Brown, went to Newton, he found a town vacation school. By asking questions he found that his church was supposed to support the school financially and to send its boys and girls. However, it seemed strange to him that the church had nothing to say about the curriculum or about the teachers. But enthusiasm ran high because the merchants of the town gave both treats and publicity. Mr. Brown discovered that two women were given complete charge of everything. They decided what was to be taught and did the teaching. In this case the church may have supported this venture, but the vacation church school did not belong to the church. What was done with the children was in many respects contrary to the church's philosophy of Christian education.

The Philosophy of Christian Education — What is the philosophy of Christian education on which the Protestant churches build their program for boys and girls? Surely there is good reason for the kind of church-school work that is recommended by our various denominations. Some

59

adults with pleasant memories may look back on their early days and question why church school is so different now. Some people, who would not think of going back to the horse and buggy for transportation or to the town pump for water, sometimes return to the old way of teaching the three R's and religion. Usually this is done because these persons do not understand the philosophy that underlines educational work with boys and girls today.

Christian Education Is Based on Needs and Is Graded — Christian education begins with the needs of people, and these needs differ with each age level. Five-year-old Sharon needs to learn to work and play with others, to find satisfaction in taking turns and being part of a group. Sharon will be helped to know Jesus as one who loved children, a friend and helper to everyone, and as one who taught people about God's love and care. But Sharon's thirteen-year-old sister, Beth, has already learned these things about Jesus, and she has already had many experiences in being a contributing member of a group. Now Beth is learning how Jesus met opposition as he both demonstrated and taught the way of love. Beth discovers that Jesus so firmly believed this was God's way for life that he refused to depend upon violence or force and stood for the way of love though it meant his death. This more mature thought of Jesus challenges Beth to dedicate her life to loving service as his follower.

We see, then, that the church's program has to be graded if it meets the needs of both Sharon and Beth. In this case each was taught about Jesus on her own level of maturity. When the vacation church school belongs to the church, it fits into this same graded approach to meet the needs of boys and girls of the church.

United in Purpose — All parts of the church program gain effectiveness when united in achieving certain purposes. A family united in the purpose of buying and building a home will work both together and individually to achieve this end. They will give up some vacations and take on odd jobs as they unite their efforts to reach their desired goal, a new home.

A church also has goals to be achieved, fruits in Christian living to be attained, and the church works for these same purposes in every part of its program. The vacation church school may provide ways of working toward these goals that are even more effective than the shorter sessions on Sunday, but the objectives remain the same.

While the reader may be aware of the needs of boys and girls that should underlie all Christian education and of objectives based on these needs, still it may serve a helpful purpose to consider these goals of Christian education. The following statement from the 1950 Yearbook of the International Council of Religious Education represents the co-operative thinking of many denominations and the basis on which curricula for many denominations are prepared. (Contact the Division of Christian Education, National Council of Churches, for their latest statements.)

1. To make God a reality in human experience; to give individuals a sense of personal relationship to him.

2. To develop an understanding and appreciation of the personality, life, and teachings of Jesus.

3. To foster Christlike character through progressive and continuous development.

4. To make the fatherhood of God and the brotherhood of man the motivation underlying the social order.

5. To develop in growing persons the disposition and the ability to participate in the organized society of Christians—the Church.

6. To develop in growing persons an appreciation of the meaning and importance of the Christian family, and the ability and disposition to participate in and contribute constructively to the life of this primary social group.

7. To lead all into recognizing God's purpose and plan in life and in the universe, and into appreciating each person's essential part in God's plan.

8. To help man assimilate the best religious experience of the race, pre-eminently that recorded in the Bible, as the guide to present experience.[1]

How Children Learn and Grow — There must be ways of achieving goals. One seldom reaches a destination without knowing where he is going, but he also needs to face the problem of how to get there. In order to realize Christian education goals we recognize that learning and growing are inseparable. All the time one is growing, he is learning. All the time one is learning, he is growing. Both are changes that take place gradually. When we say one learns, we are assuming change—change in ways of thinking, in attitudes, in conduct, and in skills. All of these are interwoven in experiences.

What Are Growing Persons Like? — The importance of experience as a means of learning is rooted in the nature of the persons whom we teach. The church's program should be built on an understanding of the boys and girls for which any part of the program is planned. It should ask and answer the questions: What are these growing persons like? How do they learn and grow? What is this process of growth which God has set up within the person and with which man must co-operate?

First, the child has physical, mental, emotional, and social needs that must be understood and satisfied if he is to develop wholesomely. This should be obvious, but many who work with growing boys and girls do not understand this wholeness of the person. His mental development cannot be parceled out to the public school, his spiritual development to the church, and his physical development to the home. The whole self develops together, and every

---

[1] From the International Council of Religious Education Yearbook 1950 printed by The International Council of Religious Education 1950 now a part of the National Council of Churches. Used with permission.

experience the growing person has teaches him something, whether or not this is what we would choose to have him learn. An understanding of the child's total needs rather than thinking merely of his spiritual needs would help church leaders in reaching their goals of Christian teaching. It would also help them solve many of the problems they now have with individual children and youth.

The Child Is Always Active — To understand the growing child is to discover that he is always active. It is what he does when confronted with things, with persons, and with situations that determines what he learns. If the child were merely passive—a sponge soaking up influence, information, and habits of behavior—he would not be the living, growing persons he is. It is what the child does with the "stuff" of life, what he actively absorbs and assimilates from the life about him, that counts in his growing and learning. He experiments with life and enjoys or rejects each part of it.

The Child Learns What He Practices—When children are young, they imitate what they see and hear. They experiment and learn through their senses. They enjoy or repulse all that comes to them in these ways. Repeating the satisfying experiences and avoiding those that make boys and girls unhappy, tend to develop a pattern of behavior. As children grow, they increasingly think about all they see and hear, and these thoughts are never entirely separated from their feelings—in fact, they are greatly influenced by them.

As a growing boy or girl participates in life and its activities, he practices certain ways of doing and living. He learns what he practices of his own accord, whether it is good or bad. We try to help him want to practice what is good for him and society—to find satisfaction in practicing the good ways of life. Here again we have to recall that the whole person acts, for when the body is active, the mind and the emotions are active, too.

63

Feelings accompany every physical experience, furnishing the drive or serving to check the interest. Mental activity both serves to help the person respond to life and stimulates further activity. Such activity may be characterized by perceiving, remembering, imagining, integrating, or reasoning. Insights and meanings, so much a part of religion, come through this combination of physical, mental, and emotional activity. The whole self is involved, and any effective commitment to any way of life must come through the active learnings of the whole self. To understand the child in this way is infinitely significant to the religious leader.

A Favorable Growing Climate — When we think of growth and learning in these ways, we realize that Christian nurture cannot wait until the child is a certain age and that it cannot be limited to once-a-week Sunday sessions. If a climate favorable for spiritual growth and development is needed from birth, then part of the church's task is to help the home in providing a favorable atmosphere for Christian nurture. Indeed, it cannot even stop there for the whole environment teaches. But the home and church can begin early to help the child develop some basic Christian values. These must begin with parents—parents who love each other and their children and who lovingly seek the will and purposes of God for themselves and their family. This is the basic influence.

The church can supplement what the home does and dramatize its importance when it takes its task seriously, allocates enough time, energy, and support, and when it exercises enough effort and wisdom to discharge this responsibility. It should be emphasized, however, that action is necessary by all involved in the teaching. The church, itself, must have a unified approach to growing boys and girls, and it must be a co-operative agent with the home and other constructive influences or agencies. Otherwise much of its effort and influence will be lost.

An illustration may be useful in clarifying how the nature of the child and the way he learns determine the philosophy and practice of Christian education. Let us see how it works out in an effort to achieve one of our purposes in Christian education, namely, a growing relationship with God. Think what it means to grow in such a relationship! It is much more than learning to talk about God or even to God. Learning to say words about God or to God is much less significant than a feeling and thinking response to God. A relationship is something to be lived, not just thought about, not just talked about, not just to have feelings about, and not just a physical activity of bowing the head or knee. A living relationship involves the whole self.

Words Are Symbols — At this point it is well to remember that words are symbols—they stand for something, but they have little meaning to children until they are made meaningful through experience. What do you suppose it means to a very young child to say that God is love? If we can divorce each word from the experiences we as adults have associated with these words, they are mere sounds. Much of what we say to children are mere sounds, not meanings. We get nearer the child when we say that God is loving like a father, but even then, to have meaning, the child must have the experience of a loving father who demonstrates that loving means being kind and thoughtful.

It is only when a child experiences what the words imply and is able to associate the words with the experiences that words serve a useful purpose. It is a waste of precious opportunity to base so much of our teaching on the telling method. One can only grow in relationship to God as he experiences God's living presence, his creative wonders, and his loving purposes, and then responds to them. It takes the home and the church both to provide adequate opportunity for such experiences.

Growing persons increasingly evaluate the consequences of

what they do and observe. They learn to select more important values. A young child will ask for a nice day for a picnic,
but increasingly he comes to appreciate that God works
in his world through dependable laws. The child must
be mature enough to read weather maps and see the relationship between high and low pressure areas and wind
flow, to appreciate a God whose laws are dependable and
intelligible. Each age level has its own needs for religion,
not just to get ready for adulthood, but to live richly during
the growing years.

The maturing of experience and the difference it makes
may be illustrated in another incident. Brian, who is five,
and Paul, who is eleven, are both interested in Christmas,
and both ask questions that lead to some interpretation of
the Christmas experience. At five Brian needs to feel the
mystery and the wonder of life. The birth of the baby
Jesus with all the reverent celebration of the event helps
Brian have this enriching religious feeling. But Paul at
eleven is thinking, "What does it mean?" Paul needs an
interpretation of the experience. He is mature enough to
understand what a difference it would make in the world
if love were practiced. Christmas is a time when we remind
ourselves of the great leadership of Jesus in the practice
of love and good will. This is the reason we observe his
birthday for it was Jesus who helped the world know God's
way of love in living. Jesus, himself, is an expression of the
love of God.

In Paul's case verbal interpretation of the Christmas experience plays a part in his learning. Many overrate the part
it plays, but it does have its place. When boys and girls
seek information, they are most ready to receive it. Mere
telling by an adult, apart from the related experience, is
often wasted effort.

What Is Christian Education? — This is a question to be
answered by every Christian educator—everyone concerned
with the program of Christian nurture: parents, church-

school teachers, ministers, boards of Christian education. We have to decide whether the Christian religion is a quality of life that transforms life in all its relationships because it is a commitment to God as we know him through Jesus, or if the Christian religion is a set of beliefs and practices to be transmitted to each succeeding generation.

Many ministers, teachers, and parents accept the former as basic, in which case the primary concern is not subject matter (except as material to be used). The emphasis is on the moral and spiritual growth of persons. Persons grow when they experience moral and spiritual values in real living and have opportunity to interpret values as they live them out in experience. It is that kind of living that the church tries to make possible whether in the church building, in the home, on the playground, or at a place of work. One cannot learn to live except by living.

Group Values and Opportunities — There are opportunities for positive learning from group relationships that should be a challenge to church-school leaders. Most people are gregarious, but the trend in our population points toward the need for learning to live with greater numbers of other people. Boys and girls in church school are learning in a group. No two boys and girls will get the same result because each will have a different relationship to the group. Each person brings something different within himself to the classroom. Each person, therefore, will have a different learning and will attach a different meaning to his experiences at the church.

Does the child feel at home, welcomed, and needed by other members of the group? Boys and girls need to feel that they are welcomed by the teacher as well as to feel welcomed by the group. Yet children can feel welcome only when they receive recognition from the group, when they feel adequate to the demands of the occasion and can participate in what others are doing because it is on their own level of intelligence and capability. Boys and girls do not have to show off to get the attention of the group or to make themselves felt when their ideas and achievements are respected. This group relationship not only makes a difference in how a person feels, but the way he feels will make a great difference in what he learns.

The Vacation Church School—A Learning Situation — The vacation church school offers blocks of time for living together from which Christian relationships may be learned. Here is truly an opportunity for learning through experiences. As boys and girls are studying, singing, looking up references, worshiping, working, or playing together, they are living and working with one another and with the teacher. The enthusiasm of the teacher and of the group for what they are doing will help determine the attitudes that are learned. But the teacher cannot just bubble enthusiasm. There must be work to do which boys and girls help plan, in which they feel a sense of achievement, and in which they become a fellowship working together toward some worth-while, self-determined goal.

The influence of the group on one's learning should not be difficult to perceive. It is the group morale that often determines the standard of conduct for the individual. What the group likes may influence the individual's attitude. When group behavior is commendable, the individual who experiences it in the group may be influenced in his own behavior when away from the group.

There are other advantages in group learning. While every person is different from every other, yet those of the same age face similar problems. One cannot always make a direct approach to personal problems, but as groups work with situations similar to their own, the individual boy or girl may recognize his own problem and make application to himself. Sometimes one recognizes his problem, but does not know how to solve it. He may learn through the group's solution in a similar situation. Leaders learn about the personal strengths and weaknesses of boys and girls as they are manifested through group work. This happens when a wise leader offers a self-centered pupil an opportunity to experience the joy that comes to him in group planning for and sharing in some unselfish service to others.

The Socialized Classroom — In recent years public education places a new emphasis on the importance of group life. Teaching has been changing from formal recitations to more socialized classrooms in which there is a friendly spirit of co-operative work. The teacher exercises leadership as a working member of the group instead of an upfront person, the great authority and dictator. While the group plans, makes decisions, assumes and discharges responsibilities, and evaluates its work, the role of the teacher is that of consultant and adviser. The teacher suggests and demonstrates a good working relationship. Such a teacher must learn to be a co-operative person who stimulates a desire on the part of the pupils to achieve certain goals and to want to struggle toward the solution of life's problems.

This kind of teacher must know and understand boys and girls and their social experiences outside the classroom. The teacher needs to have a genuine desire to help pupils understand themselves and to develop Christian relationships in their concern for one another and all other people. The atmosphere of the classroom must be permissive enough for each one to be a contributing member, free to experiment and discover what he can offer as a partner in co-operative living.

This changing attitude in education aims at increased activity on the part of the pupil in which he develops self-confidence, self-reliance, assumes responsibility, gets training in initiative, independence of thought, ability to adapt himself to others, to respect the abilities of others, and to practice self-judgment while he evaluates a piece of work. The disciplines are inherent in such a process, not just something to be discussed. The task to be done becomes the center of plans and activity. This is the reason the church needs the vacation church school. It is set up to provide the kinds of experience needed for practicing life's disciplines.

Conclusions — Learning and growing take place in guided experiences through which wise leaders help boys and girls work out problems in relationships with others, practice the disciplines involved in good work, make discoveries that pertain to their own lives and which lead to wise choices and deepened insight. No two pupils will learn the same things from what happens in a group, but each will be learning something. The leader who hopes to give careful guidance will need to keep the group small enough to work with individuals yet large enough for effective relationships to develop and purposeful enough to meet the religious needs of the group. There must also be time enough for the group to plan and carry out learning activities.

Time Enough for Learning — Christian education recognizes the need for more time for learning. Learning is a slow process. The church that recognizes this will make possible day-by-day sessions with enough time so that growing and learning experiences can be guided. Teachers in Sunday sessions often find that time is a very limiting factor, making it difficult for their boys and girls to take part in planning. It also takes time to discover and investigate, listen, read, experiment, and use what information is discovered. But this is a part of learning. It is lack of time that often prevents the enrichment which could come from pupil planning and doing and from using additional resources. The vacation church school provides more time for the use of books and pictures, for interviewing interesting people, and for trips to the public library, or to a settlement house, or to other churches.

Creative activity is an important part of learning in the vacation church school. Time is required to dramatize, read stories, create litanies, write psalms, sing hymns, serve the needs of others, reach across the world in missionary enterprises, and record one's findings and learning in some useful and artistic way. All such activity can stretch the imagination and spirit, and can bear rich fruits in Christian love and understanding. But many churches are poverty-stricken for lack of time on Sunday morning to do this kind of creative teaching to enrich the learnings of boys and girls.

Total Planning— The vacation church school is just one important part of the church's total ministry to children and youth as it builds on what happens in the Sunday school. Of course, it would be an advantage to have the same teacher for all of these enriching experiences. A limited short Sunday session should cause a teacher to want to continue with the same group in the vacation church school thus definitely tying the two together. Not only does the vacation church school extend the teaching time, but many of the experiences of either school may be used as a basis for further work in the other. Too often it is impossible for one leader to work with the same boys and girls both on Sunday and through the week. The question then will be asked, "How can we keep all parts of our church program integrated?" One way to do this is to have all leaders who work with a group plan together.

Let us illustrate with fourth-grade pupils what is meant by total planning. Third graders often receive Bibles as they are promoted into the fourth grade or junior department. Their Sunday church-school lessons may be organized around this experience, that is, learning to use the Bible, finding out how the Bible is distributed throughout the world, getting acquainted with certain portions of the Bible, using it in worship, and as a guide to living.

Let us suppose that the vacation church school emphasis for the current year is on "Personal and Group Relationships." This unit would develop Christian attitudes and actions in all relations with others—home, church, school, and community. In the same year suppose the church camp for juniors is emphasizing evidences of God's work. The current mission study may be "Mexican Neighbors."

Such a mixture looks far from integrated! It would be much simpler if the same teacher of junior boys and girls could counsel in the camp, teach in the Sunday and vacation church schools, and guide the mission study. This continuing experience would permit a teacher to know the boys and girls well enough to meet their needs as individuals, to relate the learning from all these sources, and to follow up needs and ideas of the children that are revealed from time to time. Resource leaders could be brought in as needed. But when there are different teachers for different occasions, they will need to plan and work together long enough to achieve these same values. Each leader will not only know what happens to Johnny in Sunday school or vacation church school or junior choir, but each teacher will share with the others to such an extent that all will know Johnny's needs, evaluate his work in the various groups, and mark his progress. This takes close co-operation. How is it obtained?

How Leaders Co-operate— The department superintendent of the church school should be the correlating person who calls together all the workers with pupils of a department. The total picture showing various emphases and various opportunities should be placed before all the workers, and they should ask themselves, "How can we give these boys and girls a growing, progressing wholeness of learning that gathers up and unifies their church experiences?"

The choir director might answer this question by saying that he can use music that correlates with the lesson materials. As he and the other leaders look over the music needed, he will be able to decide which will be most usable for special numbers. The Sunday church-school teacher, the vacation church school teacher, and the mission-study teacher may need to look at their courses together to find ways in which the work can be correlated. For instance, while the Sunday-school teacher is guiding fourth, fifth, and sixth graders to see how the Bible was sent to all the world, he might encourage them to investigate whether or not Bibles are needed in any specific place by contacting denominational channels and the American Bible Society. Or, it may be the mission-study leader who does this, knowing that the boys and girls have been especially interested in learning how Bibles go to various parts of the world. It may be that the vacation church school is the only one providing enough time actually to plan and carry out the project in which they will get the money to provide Bibles for other children.

This is a simple and limited illustration, but it suffices to show that when people plan together to solve a common problem, the pupil benefits. It is for this reason that pupils belong to the church family. They have a right to expect that the church plans for them in a total way so that every learning experience contributes to every other learning experience. When the vacation church school is part of the total plan and fits into the picture in this way, then it really belongs to the church. Any steps in this direction will prove their worth even where total integration cannot be achieved.

Co-operative Planning With Other Churches — Co-operative planning for a vacation church school is still more complicated when the church co-operates with other churches. How can this total planning be done when other churches are involved in it? Getting together the leaders of any one age group of all the churches is not easy and not always practical. But as the local church participates in the planning of a community school, it has a part in making decisions. It needs to be there when the emphases for the vacation church school are selected. Any particular age-

73

group representatives from the various churches should go over these materials. In this way leaders discover what experiences the children need just the same as if their church held its own school.

Evaluation— Because the vacation church school belongs to the church and is a part of the total program, there should be a serious evaluation of it. (See Chapter 12.) The evaluation should be in terms of the purposes that were set up in advance. Were these purposes achieved? Purpose is a great ally of achievement. Or, perhaps the weakness has been lack of contact with parents, and this is brought out in the evaluation. Leaders who think beyond the vacation church school to the whole church then ask themselves, "Has this neglect been true in our total program? Does the fact that we find it a weakness in the vacation church school also point out that it is a weakness in the rest of our church work?" Through this kind of evaluation the vacation church school helps the church see its task and do its work most effectively. Recommendations through the board of Christian education should influence future planning in the total program, for the vacation church school belongs to the church!

Summary — The vacation church belongs when it is regularly scheduled, written into the church budget, and built into the church's philosophy of education.

The philosophy of Christian education says that Christian education is based on pupil needs and is graded; that all phases of the church's program need to be united in purpose; that persons learn and grow through living life rather than by merely talking about it; that living and learning involve the whole person in home, church, and community; that the program is concerned about a quality of life that transforms living; that group life has values and opportunities for Christian growth.

The church needs the vacation church school to provide

the place and time needed for group living and learning.

Co-operative planning is needed to unify the church's approach to persons and to conserve the benefits of its total program.

Education and psychology affirm that a pupil learns best what he has a chance to practice; that he learns what he does and what he feels and thinks as he does it; that growth comes as each individual has a chance to realize and develop his own talents and potential abilities; that unused energy, unused talents, and unused ideas are a waste to both society and the kingdom of God; also a means of frustrating the individual, causing him to be maladjusted; that pupils learn more than one thing at a time, for they are learning through the mind, emotions, and sense impressions; that a leader cannot give learning to a pupil, for he learns only by his own activity, his participation is essential, and he learns to the degree in which he wholeheartedly participates.

The Bible affirms that the whole self is involved in learning and growing (Luke 2:52); that it is what one does with the stuff of life that counts (John 6:8-11); that religion is important on each age level (Mark 10:15); that the teacher needs to prepare (2 Timothy 2:15).

Suggestions for Things to Do

1. What mutual support exists between the various phases of your church program?

2. Select a boy or a girl of your acquaintance (or from your church) and list his church relationship, such as Sunday church-school department, class, choir, Scouts or other clubs, church fellowship or society groups, vacation church school, missionary groups.

Answer the following questions about the church program for this boy or girl:

a) What overlapping (or correlation) is there in the activities, units of work and study, service projects, worship, and recreation?

75

b) Which groups does he like best and why?

c) How does his behavior and interest differ in the various groups?

d) How many leaders are involved in this person's church experiences?

e) What planning do the leaders do together?

f) Suggest steps toward total planning for this boy or girl.

The Vacation Church School Belongs

TO THE COMMUNITY

Winfield is an average town. At the January ministerial meeting the chairman mentioned that he had already received denominational materials setting forth the values of early planning for next summer's vacation church school. Discussion began when he said: "I just wondered if we could do anything together this year. So far, each church has gone its own way, but we all seem to have problems. One problem is that there is a great deal of competition for the children's time."

Conflicts Are Serious — Conflicts with the public-school summer sessions that ran through the month of June were considered a serious handicap by all the ministers at the meeting. One minister had held his vacation church school in July the preceding year instead of the usual month of June. July was found to be a much better time as far as conflicting with summer school was concerned, but there was a conflict with the recreation programs sponsored by the City Parks and Recreation Department. These conflicting programs in Winfield meant that some boys and girls had many activities from which to choose during one part of the summer and nothing to do at other times.

The ministers took the initiative in calling together representatives from all the agencies of the city who might be making up a schedule of summer activities for children and youth. Representatives came from the public schools, Boy Scouts, Camp Fire Girls, Y.M.C.A., Y.W.C.A., the City Parks and Recreation Department, and churches. In working on a joint summer schedule these persons found some unavoidable overlapping of dates because camp dates could not be changed as there were no other times available at the camp sites. Co-operative planning had begun, however, that resulted in a Winfield summer calendar as follows:

June	July	August
Public school summer sessions, 8:00 A.M.- 11:00 A.M.	Vacation church school, 8:30 A.M.- 11:00 A.M. held in several churches.	Crafts, stories, and dramatics in parks under the City Parks and Recreation Department.
Swimming pool, 11:00 A.M.- 11:50 A.M. Open to children.	Swimming pool, 11:00 A.M.- 11:50 A.M. Open to children.	Swimming pool, 11:00 A.M.- 11:50 A.M. Open to children.

Afternoon recreational programs were scheduled for all summer. Swimming, archery, and ball games were encouraged. In the evenings there were free movies in the parks, ball games, a few concerts, and many picnics.

Winfield's joint plan was an improvement over previous years, but it was far from adequate. Some children missed the vacation church schools entirely because camps and day camps were heavily scheduled in July. Furthermore, no part of the program entirely covered the city. There were two or three vacation church schools in some areas of the city and none in others. There were neither parks nor playgrounds in the downtown area, and yet many people lived there. One end of town seemed completely left out.

Representatives from the various churches and other social agencies of the city met early in the fall to see if overlapping and neglect could be avoided the second summer. The Salvation Army, the P.T.A., and several service clubs joined with the original planners. Many faults in the first plan were corrected, and this joint planning resulted in less conflict with the camp program by a staggered schedule for vacation church schools. This plan spread the schools over more of the summer and covered more of the city, and made a wider use of recreational facilities.

Co-operation Demonstrated— It took some intensive planning for the churches and the City Parks and Recreation Department to spread their programs to more parts of the city and over more of the summer. All vacation church schools were provided with play equipment and playground leadership for part of the time by the City Parks and Recreation Department. In turn, churches solicited leaders from their membership to help with the park programs of crafts, dramatics, and story hours. While one area would be having a vacation church school, another might be having an intensive recreational program. Helped by both the churches and the recreational leaders, the youth of the city joined through the Y.M.C.A. and the Y.W.C.A. in evening music and dramatic programs held in the parks. Co-operative work with young people made a rather weak start the first summer, but it grew in popularity and strength in succeeding years.

The Winfield picture lifts up both some problems and some benefits that may come to boys and girls when the vacation church school seeks to become a part of the community. What at first seemed to be a problem of conflicting interests was later seen to be much less of a problem than the need to provide all children and youth with enriching experiences all summer. Churches found out that it was only in co-operation that they could undertake to cover the whole city with vacation church schools. They had to pool their resources of leadership, finances, buildings, and equipment. And the vacation church schools had to be scheduled in such a way as to fit into a summer schedule planned by the various groups concerned for the welfare of all the boys and girls.

Thinking of Children's Needs — The churches of a community must consider the needs of all the boys and girls of the community. It is not enough to plan only for those of church-related families. Churches are members of communities, owing spiritual ministry to the community and therefore under necessity of finding ways of serving every boy and girl. This moral obligation can be partly discharged by providing vacation church schools that offer Christians a means of expressing their concern for boys and girls in all kinds of places and conditions. The vacation church school offers Christian nurture to the youth of suburban residence communities or in transient, downtown areas of large cities. Vacation church schools may be conducted before, after, or between harvesttime in rural areas or during the harvest for children in migrant camps. There may be an all-summer vacation church school program in a trailer town that has few other enriching experiences for its youth. All children have a right to adequate Christian nurture regardless of their location or their living circumstances.

Vacation Church Schools Can Belong to the Community — One way in which the vacation church school can belong to the community is to adapt itself to the needs and conditions in the community. In rural communities, for instance, distances may be great enough to justify longer days and a fewer number of weeks. Evening sessions may be the answer, especially where other religious educational opportunities are limited for older members of the families. The combination of fellowship and learning is characteristic of many organizations of our times. A mother's club may meet in connection with a vacation church school wherever it is possible to do so.

Belonging to the Community When Churches Work Together — Ministerial associations often make it possible for churches to work together within a given area. These are both denominational and interdenominational. Both have their place, but communities are not adequately organized to maintain Christian education for all persons unless there is interdenominational co-operation. When co-operation for Christian education purposes starts with ministers, it often develops into an organization that includes lay people. As ministers develop such a program, there is soon need for other leaders to participate.

A council of churches may be the organization that enables churches to work together. Churches can maintain vacation church schools to meet the needs of the community when they voluntarily associate themselves just for this purpose. More often the council of churches is on a year-round basis. A council of this kind may be organized on a county, city, or district basis so that its member churches can minister to the whole community instead of being limited to their immediate neighborhoods and memberships.

When there is an ongoing organization of this kind, there is usually a committee on summer activities for boys and girls, or a vacation church school committee, or both. Such committees, serving on an annual basis, will study the needs of their communities and plan together to meet those needs, pooling their resources and leadership, and stimulating and helping one another to reach out to include more people more of the time.

Such an ongoing organization for co-operative service gives a core of strength to united effort, making it more secure and enduring. Such a demonstration of unity enlists community respect and makes it possible for churches to share in the corporate life of the community. A council of churches has many advantages as it enlarges the scope of work and influence of its member churches. Just as an individual is a greater help in a cause when he belongs to a group organized for a common purpose, so is the church making a stronger impact on the community when associating with other churches to achieve common purposes.

What Co-operation Can Do — It is the experience of many communities that there will be more summer opportunities

81

when churches and other agencies concerned about the needs of people study their local needs, plan together, and co-operate in seeing that boys and girls are served. It will make possible better planning, and there will be less competition on concentrated dates because there will be a spreading out of dates to make a continuous offering through the summer. The needs of a community and of those boys and girls most often neglected will be more adequately fulfilled. Another result of such co-operation is earlier planning often preceded by some kind of united study and evaluation of the total needs and former program.

Types of Vacation Church Schools — Understanding the various types of vacation church schools provides a basis for seeing how churches may co-operate and the nature of their participation.

1. *The Individual Church Vacation School.* This type is planned by one local church. It is staffed and supported by that local church and usually (not always) is planned for the children of its membership and immediate community. Local churches can plan together for individual schools so as to reach all children in a community. They may train leaders together. Some programs might be shared, too, thus giving churches the benefit of one another's thinking and resources.

2. *The Co-operative Denominational Vacation Church School.* This type may be sponsored, planned, supported, and conducted by two or more churches of one denomination. This co-operative effort is jointly planned, and the responsibilities are shared. Leadership and finances may be pooled. The pooling of space may depend on the locations of the churches with reference to one another and to the boys and girls. Some communites heavily populated with children may be served by the neighborhood church with the help of another church of the same denomination located elsewhere.

3. *The Interdenominational Vacation Church School.*

82

This type consists of two or more churches of more than one denomination. Most communities have several churches representing different denominations. All churches reap the benefits of a vacation church school in the community, and all churches should share the responsibilities, whether or not they can individually provide adequate space, leadership, or financial support to conduct their own school. Some churches prefer to co-operate because they enjoy the rich fellowship in co-operation. They are able to do better work together, and they can more adequately serve the needs of the community.

Wherever there is community planning, there is a trend toward interdenominational co-operation. It should be noted in this connection that the vacation church school movement has started increased co-operation among denominations. Training institutes for vacation church school leadership are typically interdenominational. As we look further at instances of co-operation and co-ordination, we shall see that by working together churches are better able to fit into the plans of the rest of the community. They are also better able to serve areas that are either unchurched or that have limited church facilities. The quality of service is lifted when the finances, leadership, and other resources are combined in this common interest.

Emphasis should always be placed on reaching boys and girls of a community with the best possible vacation church schools. Some large schools, centrally located, co-operative, and interdenominational, can blind us to real conditions. Because the school is large, it is easy to conclude that most of the boys and girls of the community are served. It may be necessary to have more schools scattered over more areas and scheduled for more periods in order to serve the needs of children and youth. A community survey helps reach all.

Community Co-ordination—A Growing Trend— There is a growing trend toward community co-ordination in planning for children and youth of a neighborhood or city. In many cases the participation of churches seems very incidental, but in other cases the churches either have initiated such community planning and activity or are actively participating in it as in the Winfield case cited in this chapter. Such participation is always hampered by groups who are unwilling to make changes from their traditional dates or patterns, such as insisting on having the vacation school the following two weeks after school closes.

Co-ordination means a willingness on the part of all to co-operate to make possible the least conflict of competing interests, the widest coverage of all boys and girls of the area with wholesome summer opportunities, and the willingness to share leadership, space, supplies, equipment. In short, it is a co-operative effort to meet the needs of the greatest number of boys and girls for as much of the summer as possible in order to fill their leisure hours with worthwhile and meaningful experiences.

Community co-ordination is implemented by such groups as welfare councils, neighborhood councils, regional councils of health and welfare, councils of social agencies, community centers, P.T.A. groups, ministerial associations, and councils of churches. All such agencies have many common purposes for the services they give to people. Many and varied forms of community study and co-operation may be found. There is no attempt to report here any one pattern as best, but rather to indicate some ways in which the various agencies get together, their reasons for co-ordination, and the implications for churches and vacation church schools.

Reports of Community Co-ordination — The following excerpts from reports of community co-ordination will indicate some reason for group study and service, the nature of the co-operation, and some of the implications for follow-up. The first comes from a large city and surrounding county in the Great Lakes area:[1]

---

[1] From "Day Camp and Summer Program Study." Used by permission of the Council of Social Agencies, Buffalo, New York.

A committee conducting a study of day camps recognized the need to consider other types of summer program resources . . . . consequently, the study
was extended to cover various types of summer programs available for children and youth from three to
seventeen. Churches that operated day camps and
summer programs for their brotherhood or community were included in the study.

The report of the study committee included findings concerning day camps and other summer programs in regard to:

number of children and youth served
services to exceptional children
program, policy, procedures, leadership training
geographical areas served

Included among recommendations of the committee were
the following:

extension of day camp and other summer program
activities
consideration of undeserved areas in extending
summer programs
joint planning by agencies and possible joint operation of program in some areas
provision for exceptional children (physically, men-
tally, emotionally, handicapped)
provision for reporting summer programs to public
schools
suggestions for length of season, camp sites, standards

A School and Community Recreation Program — In a South-
east community a grant was made by the state to a city for
an extended school program. It is interesting to note the
way in which the public school planned with other agencies
of the city in setting up this summer program:[2]

Planning by the school was begun early in co-
operation with the recreation board, Y.M.C.A.,

---

[2] Used by permission of the City Schools of Decatur, Decatur, Georgia.

Scouts, library, P.T.A., Red Cross, service league, and church representatives. The schools had a precedent of working with various groups in sharing school facilities and grounds. All of these groups had some sort of summer activity that provided a wide variety of services. The school's aim was to supplement and enrich rather than duplicate. . . . The various groups planned jointly for such things as scheduling, places to meet, equipment, supplies, policies, and activities. When the program was agreed upon the participating groups met weekly to evaluate and plan for the next week. All groups and participants shared in the final evaluation and received copies of the final report. Since vacation church schools were already scheduled, other activities were planned around their date.

Money for the extended school program was not allocated except the one year, but there is still overall planning between various groups. This includes such things as clearing dates for vacation church schools and delegating various responsibilities: e.g., Little Theatre to the recreation board; day camping to the Y.M.C.A.; Scouts and story hour to the library; teaching of swimming to the Red Cross.

An Interfaith Vacation School — A community council in an Illinois town had been dealing with civic problems, such as flood control. The work is reported as follows:

There was representation from various community groups including Protestant churches and Roman Catholic churches. In one meeting a leader suggested, "Our next undertaking should be doing something for the children." Everyone was aware of serious tensions between the children who attended the public school and those who attended the large Roman Catholic parochial school in the community. Plans were made for a vacation school in which two faith groups co-operated. Leadership was drawn from professional and lay workers in both groups. It was understood that certain aspects of a summer program could not be carried on together, such as many kinds of worship experiences, but there were many areas in which it would be possible to plan together. A summer program was developed including activities, recreation, and story hours. This was carried on with great satisfaction both to the leaders and to the boys and girls. Tensions were replaced by friendly attitudes and experiences as individuals of the two faith groups came to know one another through focusing on a common interest.

The Vacation Church School Uses Community Resources — *The Public Library.* This is one source for mutually enriching the vacation church school and the community. Most librarians would be happy to make the library's resources of books, pictures, magazines, slides, films, and records available for use in vacation church schools. But librarians can do this only when the leader gives information regarding the theme to be emphasized, a list of the units to be used by the various age groups and a suggested list of reading and audio-visuals needed. Perhaps it is some listening music wanted in a worship unit or stories of musicians and church leaders. Recall the teachers in Chapter 3 who wanted to find out how a shepherd's pipe is made. The librarian took as much pride in finding that description as if she had written it.

Many libraries carry films recommended in vacation church school teaching materials. Some of these come from public education sources. Some libraries carry films produced for religious education by denominational and interchurch agencies. Churches that do not have facilities for playing records or showing films frequently go to the library for special showings.

Lists of reading books correlating with the theme of the vacation church school will be made up by many librarians and put on special display to attract young readers. One junior-high church-school teacher planned with the librarian for a research session at the library. The teacher was surprised to find that the librarian had the appropriate reference books conveniently spread out on tables with markers to indicate where the information would be found.

Long before a vacation church school starts, teachers begin their preparation. After reading the unit in their textbooks they should explore other community resources. Libraries full of available resources are often overlooked.

Newspapers. Another way mutually to enrich the vacation church school and the community is through newspaper service. Newspapers do serve the churches when they give publicity to vacation church schools, but the churches serve the newspapers and through them the community when they provide news items about the schools. Unchurched families sometimes send their children as a direct result of such feature stories. There is much of human interest going on in vacation church schools, and the whole attitude of a community can be influenced by such stories and good pictures.

Resources of Persons and Institutions. Many persons in a community may help vacation church schools. A doctor may visit the kindergarten to become a friend of the children. They listen through the stethoscope and share various other experiences with the doctor that make them less afraid when they are sick. An official of the railroad introduces primary boys and girls to a new interest in train travel. A fire marshal goes over the church with juniors to show ways of preventing fire hazards. A minister tells why he visits hospital patients and a "Gray Lady" tells how she helps those who cannot help themselves during their hospital stay. A conservation officer takes a trip with a group to find out ways in which the earth gives man a home. Think of the persons in any community who have something of value to share that will enrich the living of people. Community-conscious vacation church school leaders will not lightly pass up these opportunities.

The Public Schools. Public schools are more and more concerned about the long summer vacations. Many evils attend idleness and boredom. Time should be constructively used instead of wasted as it so often is in the summer. More and more school systems are making their playgrounds, play equipment, swimming pools, and shops available to the community outside school hours and in the summer. In some communities the public schools may be open eleven months of the year in the future. Each church must discover within its own community what kinds of cooperation with public schools are desirable or practical.

The Significance of Community — This chapter may well end with a reconsideration of the meaning of community and its significance for the church. We have come to use the terms community and neighborhood lightly to designate a common location or area. But the word community assumes that people commune with one another. It is a two-way process. In a true neighborhood there is neighborliness. It takes a lot of living and friendly association to make a place a community or neighborhood. A church that seeks to be an integral part of community life must be neighborly with its people, with other churches, and with all other organizations and agencies seeking the welfare of persons.

The community is a teacher of the young. It helps determine the moral standards, the kinds of influence affecting families, the educational level, and the social relationships of its people. The church can share in this teaching in two ways: directly, by its own program of teaching; indirectly, by influencing and vitalizing the community of which it is a part. The church radiates this influence as it shares in councils of churches, councils of social agencies, and as it seeks to be a uniting force. Its influence can permeate the whole structure from within better than from without. This does not mean that the church must dominate or seek always to have its own way, for Christians should make the best team workers.

When the church shares itself in the give and take of teamwork, it strengthens rather than weakens its position.

The situation is entirely different from the scriptural one, but it is not hard to imagine the Master saying as he looks over our home communities what he said when he looked over Jerusalem: "How often would I have gathered your children together . . . and you would not!" (Luke 13:34.) Let us as adults gather ourselves together so that all of our children may have the best of our combined efforts.

Summary— The vacation church school belongs to the community when there is co-operation in planning for a full summer of enriching experiences for all boys and girls; when churches demonstrate what co-operation means and can do; when people think together about the needs of boys and girls.

Ways in which the vacation church school can belong to the community are by churches working together through ministerial associations and councils of churches; by meeting community needs through various types of vacation church schools; by community co-ordination; by using community resources.

The significance of a community lies in its influence.

Suggestions for Things to Do

1. List the agencies and organizations of your community that seek the welfare of children and youth. In what ways are any or all of these organizations working together? Through what central organization or council do they jointly look at the needs of the boys and girls of your community? What plans are made to meet these needs?

2. Survey the community to discover what recreational, cultural, and religious opportunities are provided for boys and girls during the summer.

3. Spot the vacation church schools on a population map of the community. To what extent are all areas served?

4. What can the churches of your community do to provide more vacation church school opportunties for boys and girls from four to fourteen years of age?

The Vacation Church School Belongs

TO THE HOME

THE VACATION CHURCH SCHOOL BELONGS TO THE HOME. WHAT a strange thing to say! Haven't we always assumed that the vacation church school belonged to the church? Children sometimes say, "It's my vacation church school." But in what sense can it belong to the home? For the most part children are considered the responsibility of the home during the summer. This is not always a welcome responsibility.

Two mothers on a bus passed a church and noticed a big sign on the lawn announcing a vacation church school. One mother commented to the other that she was sending her children and was surely glad to get them from underfoot for a few days. The other mother said, "It makes me wish I belonged to the church so that I could send my three children." "Oh, you don't have to belong to send the children. You can send them anyway," was the reply. So plans were promptly made by these two mothers to get together to enroll the children. But there is a deeper sense in which the vacation church school belongs to and serves the home.

Consider the Needs of Families — Some churches take seriously their responsibilities to serve the needs of families. Many are eager to develop a family program. Some churches evaluate their total program in terms of what it does to help families. These churches are concerned to provide a social climate that encourages family living, to make plans for training parents, and to provide opportunity for parents to participate in planning for the children. The result will be a more adequate Christian education with the combined efforts of home, church, and community.

One of the weakest spots in Christian education is the lack of relationship between the church and the home. This neglect in the whole church program may be partly redeemed through the vacation church school where parents enter into a planning and working partnership. It is through this kind of co-operation that parents learn what Christian education should do for boys and girls and how to go about it. True, the parents may never again be satisfied with the church school that goes its own way while the home neither knows what that way is nor has anything to say about it.

Many church-school teachers are also parents. Teachers need to think of themselves as parents, too, as they assist in guiding children. As a rule parents love their children and highly esteem the child's desires and feelings. There is a close bond between them, for parents have invested themselves in their children. Parents prize every opportunity to share in the lives and activities of their children. It is important then for parents and teachers to work together in a common task, and the results are rewarding. In churches where there is a family-life education committee it may have a joint session with the vacation church school committee to consider a family emphasis in the vacation church school. If there is no such committee, the board of Christian education may well face their responsibility in this manner.

Helping Parents Teach Religion in the Home — Basic Christian nurture is rooted in the home. Parents may try to turn it over to the church, but they cannot because it is to a large degree in the family that children experience life, ask questions, find answers, and gain their attitudes. Most brides expect to learn to cook and to keep a good house; most husbands expect to work to support their families. It should be as logical to expect parents to learn to guide their children religiously as to feed them or to clothe and shelter them. The church must hold out this expectancy.

Don Parkinson

A parent shares in the activities of the children.

Can we expect the vacation church school to provide a place for training parents to do a better task in the Christian nurture of their children? Why can it not be another and perhaps a natural opportunity to offer training? Mothers, especially, are free while children are in vacation church school to attend special training classes at least two or three days of each week. A nursery with competent women to care for young children may be provided on those days. Standards should be as high here as for the church nursery group. Knowing full well that it is a tremendous task to get parents to want this training, we must still face the necessity.

More often the vacation church school will serve parents more indirectly when they are asked to help in various ways in the program and other work entailed in conducting a vacation church school.

Parents Participate— Let us ask the teacher how the parents can participate in the planning and teaching. Do you hear someone groaning, "Oh, home co-operation! I tried that once. In fact, I invited the parents to a tea, and only two came." When one expects twenty to a party, it is easy to see that two is a small return for the investment of effort, but forget the unsuccessful party and try to realize what co-operative parents might mean to a class.

A teacher working alone with a younger group often feels the need for association with other adults. Perhaps parents are lonely, too. But here are three, a teacher and two parents, who are deeply interested in the religious education of children. They can become good companions in this great quest and give one another mutual support. Here are key parents who can give the home and family viewpoint. What are their reactions to proposed plans? Tap their impressions of the needs and interests of the pupils. Encourage them to observe the class and to participate in its work as one of the group. Treat parents and their ideas

94

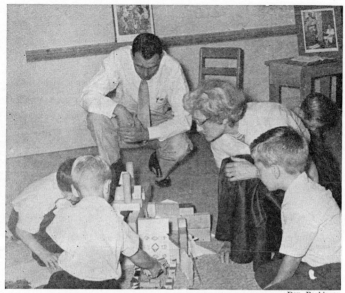

Don Parkinson

Parents may sign up to be helping teachers.

with respect and take them as far as they are willing to go into working partnership.

In advance study of a unit to be taught, a teacher may make note of questions to consider with parents. Some teachers will also make lists of possible ways in which parents might help. Before making final plans, this teacher will call together the parents for a planning and work session. Here they preview the course and its stated purposes. As parents and teachers consider these purposes, adaptation is made to the needs of the particular boys and girls to be enrolled.

Parents Sign Up for Work — The purposes to be emphasized and others to be minimized will now be ready for development. As the teacher describes possible activities and tells of needed skills in leading such activities, parents with these special skills may be enlisted to help. The teacher may also make a list of regular work to be done in which parents could give assistance. If this is on a chart or chalkboard, parents may sign up for certain times and tasks, such as playground leadership, transportation for an observation tour, projectionist for a movie to be used, photographer for a series of scenes the children may pantomime, pianist, and assistants, depending on the kinds of activities to be carried on and the needs of the local situation. There may be a similar sign-up for needed supplies, such as magazines, boxes, and other work material not supplied by the local church. Sometimes these work sessions become real work nights when parents repair or make needed furniture and equipment, such as making cupboards and bulletin boards, repairing toys, making dolls' clothes, or constructing other equipment.

It is true that many parents cannot participate during the hours of the vacation church school sessions. Fathers and mothers who are employed out of the home cannot be expected to work during the daytime. On the other hand, we often deprive employed parents of any of the joy of sharing with their children in the vacation church school just because we know they are busy and employed during the day. Can we be resourceful enough to find some time, such as an evening or Sunday afternoon, in which growing persons can have common experiences with their families? Perhaps those schools with employed parents need these common interests more than most.

Home Visitation — Home visitation is desirable. It may be possible to visit before the vacation church school begins if there is a preregistration. This is especially important in homes of new children and those whose parents are not members of the local churches. In some situations teachers may prefer to make home visits after the vacation school to help parents follow up some of the experiences the children have had. There are many reasons for home visitations: to enlist the participation and interest of parents; to extend the friendliness of the church to the unchurched; to acquaint parents with the purpose of the units to be used with their children. It is best when visits can be made by one of the teachers, but when this is impossible, interested parents make the best liaison person between the church school and the home. We have long been acquainted with the room-mother idea in public schools. This same idea has real use in the church schools, and parents may make the best contacts with other parents in behalf of the vacation church school.

It is essential to prepare if one is to make effective calls. The following guide makes a good basis for discussion as teachers and parents consider what they are to accomplish in a home visit:

GUIDE FOR CALLING IN HOMES OF PUPILS

Purposes in Calling: To know as friends the child and his family, for in this way a child comes alive as an individual and a person; to understand the child so that the school can adjust to his needs and as a basis for making the program child-centered; to enlist interest and participation of family; to gain parents' ideas and suggestions.

WHAT WE NEED TO KNOW ABOUT A CHILD	HOW TO DISCOVER
Parents' educational and cultural resources and relationship to the church	Walls and rooms talk—notebooks, magazines, records, pictures, language
What other members are in the family?	Observation or conversation
Child's interests and hobbies what he likes to do in school	Evidence of toys and pets
what he does in spare time what recreation he enjoys	Conversation with child if he is present

Does he make friends easily?	Friendly conversation with
Does child like school and his grade?	parent; do not make it a questionnaire but lead con-
What fears does the child have?	versation so this information can come naturally

Invite parents for a visiting day; arrange date, time, and where to come. Parents will want to know what the school is like so each parent signs up for a visiting day.

Inform Parents — Encourage the use of material that the child brings home. One might even leave a leaflet of suggested home activities or materials for use in family worship. Perhaps in this way parents will reveal whether or not they have family worship.

How to Make a Call — Note suggestions above. A telephone call or card may notify parent of the desire of the teacher to visit.

Clearly introduce yourself and make sure the name is understood.

State that you have come to make a call because Johnny is in your class.

Be friendly. Shyness on the part of the visitor may make parents more shy. Be genuinely interested, a friend rather than a questioner.

Vacation Church School for the Whole Family — The vacation church school serves the home when it provides the whole family with a common interest—something they can enjoy and work at together. Too many churches preach that families should do things together and then promptly divide the family as soon as it crosses the church threshold. Some few churches provide family nights, and many try to get the whole family to attend the church service. Aside from these it is only the occasional church that concentrates on providing activities of common interest to the whole family.

The vacation church schools originally started for the young, and most of them, at this writing, are for boys and girls from four to fourteen. But suppose we see how some churches include young people and adults in their vacation church school.

1. *The Family Picnic.* On the evening preceding opening day of the vacation church school whole families come together for a picnic. Before eating their picnic supper, parents and children play together in several relay games. Let us suppose the theme in the vacation church school this summer is "The Church." Each picnic table gives a charade the others are to guess. Each charade portrays some useful function or activity of the church.

Then the director cleverly announces the coming school by asking a few hard questions about the church that the vacation church school will help answer. One family dramatizes its morning scurry to get ready to go to the vacation church school in which the mother is also a teacher. When it is dark enough, pictures taken of the vacation church school the preceding year are shown, closing with the singing of hymns shown on the screen. Last minute registrations are taken while people are arriving, and plans are already made for another family occasion later in the school when the boys and girls share some of their vacation church school experiences with parents and friends.

2. *Youth Group Evening Meetings.* Most of the young people of an urban church work during the day, but attend an evening church program planned for youth. On Tuesday and Friday nights of the three-week vacation church school the young people meet from 7 to 9:30 o'clock. The time includes two fifty-minute study sessions, one on their youth society organization and plans, and the other a Bible study led by a young ministerial student home for the summer. At 8:50 there is a brief recreation period that closes with a prayer circle under the stars.

In some situations "Christian Adventure Week" comes sometime during the summer with its sessions in late after-

Oscar J. Rumpf

Developing responsibility for helping on a school picnic.

noon and evening. If this is the case, then a vacation church school class for the junior-high group would not be needed.

3. *Sunday Evening Sessions.* In a rural community such sessions are held where distances average from one to five miles. There are no Monday sessions. The Sunday evening sessions include the same group grading that is held through the week, but with parents attending the children's groups and the young people having a group of their own. The sessions for younger children are largely given to activities in which the parents can join. There is a closing program on the Sunday following the school in which the parents have roles in the dramatizations, join in the songs, and show things they have made.

4. *A Church's School of Missions.* With India as the subject of study, both the boys and girls and adults in the vacation church schools use the Friendship Press and de-

100

nominational study units. Men and women meet two evenings a week for their study on India. All groups contribute to and participate in a "Festival of India" at the close of the school. The use of movies and games as well as the new knowledge of the needs of India are enhanced by a returned missionary who contributes to their knowledge of India and its customs. She also directs their gifts to serve the needs of a church in India.

5. *An Evening Vacation School for the Family*. In one small community, classes for the entire family are held for one or two weeks in the evening from seven to nine o'clock. The school is graded, and classes for parents are held at the same time.

These five instances may serve to show some different ways in which families may participate in the vacation church school program. There are many variations of these kinds of activities. The closing sharing program by departments may be one, as noted in Chapter 4. A weekly family picnic may be just as vital a part when set up on a constructive basis.

The following principles should be observed in planning for the participation of the young people and adults:

1. Be sure that the plans and programs are developed to challenge the emerging needs of growing and maturer persons with deeper and more inclusive meanings.

2. Give adolescents and adults as well as children a democratic, active part in planning and carrying on their program.

3. There should be a growing sense of responsibility, not only for their own part of the school, but for the whole vacation church school including all ages. Young people and adults should be represented on the planning group. If they are represented on the board of Christian education, as they should be, they will have a part in many of the basic decisions concerning the policy and program of the school.

It is to be remembered that members of the church

families also have a part in the vacation church school when they serve as teachers, drivers of cars, assistants to teachers in recreation, music, or dramatic activities. To some extent parents are participants when they show an interest at home in what their boys and girls are learning and encourage them to assume their responsibilities in the school. If Junior has promised to locate and paint a wooden box for some special use at the church, his parents should encourage him in doing what he has promised. Whenever parents serve the vacation church school or participate in it, church and home ties are strengthened and the vacation church school belongs to the home, serving its needs, and strengthening its spiritual fellowship.

Unchurched Homes — But what about the homes not related to the church in any other way—unchurched homes, we call them? If boys and girls from these homes are enrolled, for which every effort should be made, special attention should be given to these families. Some churches believe in assigning additional leaders for this purpose— persons who are definitely on the vacation church school staff just as are its teachers. These visiting leaders will call on parents of the unchurched children to help them feel that their children are welcome, and to include the rest of the family in other phases of the church program. Whether or not the vacation church school provides family activities, the unchurched families may be invited to other phases of the church's program, but the surest way of interesting them is to have some family experiences in connection with the vacation church school and show friendly interest and loving concern.

Summary — The vacation church school belongs to the home because it considers the needs of families and evaluates the total program in terms of what it does to help families.

The vacation church school belongs to the home because

it helps parents teach religion and improve Christian nurture in the home.

Parents are brought into the planning and are encouraged to sign up for work in the school.

Home visitation is important to reach new children as well as keeping in touch with the church families. It is important to know the purposes in calling in order to discover the needs of children.

The vacation church school is for the whole family—boys and girls, fathers and mothers.

Suggestions for Things to Do

1. Plan and experiment with several family projects that might be related to the program of your vacation church school.

2. Set aside a visiting day to make calls in the home. Plan to train the visitors. Have them practice with one another and come to conclusions about what makes a fruitful visit.

3. Plan a vacation church school workers' conference on the topic, "Ways in which the vacation church school work of each group may lead to a religious emphasis in the home."

4. It has been generally conceded that education is increasingly concerned with helping growing boys and girls solve their own personal problems, achieve emotional stability, and understand themselves as persons. Plan ways in which parents and teachers can work together to become more sensitive to their children's needs, to help children feel wanted, and to find tasks in which they will feel useful.

The Vacation Church School Belongs

TO THE PAST, PRESENT, AND FUTURE

THE VACATION CHURCH SCHOOL BELONGS TO THE PAST. A deepening understanding of the vacation church school's history and growth results in a new appreciation of its values. It is not a fly-by-night movement that suddenly arose to meet a passing need or situation and then because of changes was no longer needed. Neither has it been maintained just because it was in existence—a ready-made organization that could be employed to carry another burden. There is something inherent in the vacation church school which has continuing values. The fiftieth anniversary of this movement was widely observed in 1951. At that time the *International Journal of Religious Education* carried a historical review of the development of the movement. Because it challenges the spirit characteristic of the whole movement some excerpts are quoted from "Fifty Years and a Future." [1]

It can never be said that vacation church schools were a scheme imposed on churches "from the top." On the contrary, they arose spontaneously in different sections and in different years as attempted answers to local problems. It is therefore no simple matter to determine the date on which vacation church schools began. During the closing years of the nineteenth and the opening years of the twentieth century, a number of attempts were made by churches and other groups to deal constructively with the summertime opportunities for education.

---

[1] By Gerald E. Knoff, January, 1951. Used by permission.

Early Experiments in Canada and the United States — Sometime during the early months of 1866 persons affiliated with the First Church of Boston became interested in using the vacation summer period in a more constructive manner. Under the auspices of this congregation there was sponsored that summer a vacation school for children. This grew eventually into a summer term of the public school.

Ten years later Montreal, Quebec, furnished what seems more accurately to be the first daily vacation Bible school. In 1877 there was a school held in that city during the summertime which included in its program hymns and songs, Bible reading and memory work, as well as such items as military drills, calisthenics, manual work, and patriotic exercises.

. . . .

The Lutheran Churches, which lay much emphasis on thorough study of the Bible and the catechism, had held daily church schools in the summer for at least a decade before the end of the century, and probably much longer.

In the little town of Hopedale, Illinois, Mrs. D. T. Miles, the wife of the Methodist pastor in that town, established what appears to be one of the first vacation church schools in the United States, in mid-May, 1894. Thirty-seven boys and girls attended the school.

. . . .

In 1900 a Congregational minister started a vacation religious day school in connection with an already established camp meeting program. Meanwhile, in New York City a similar development had sprung up at the Epiphany Baptist Church.

. . . .

The Beginning of the Movement in New York, 1901 — Dr. Robert G. Boville, executive Secretary of the New York Baptist City Mission, knew of the Montreal and Epiphany Schools and saw the possibilities in this type of Christian teaching. He enlisted the assistance of students of Union Theological Seminary as principals of these schools. One of these young men became fairly well known in his later years. His name was Harry Emerson Fosdick.

One thousand children were enrolled that summer in these schools. The program included an hour's work daily on worship, health, and Christian training, and an hour reserved for manual work and play. Making hammocks was a favorite activity among the boys and sewing and basketry among the girls.

These five schools were the beginning of the vacation church school movement.

. . . .

Dr. Boville early stated that the conscious background for these schools was: "Idle children filling the streets. Idle churches darkened and silent. Unemployed students on vacation. Idle vacation days and Children's Courts."

. . . .

Having established the movement in New York, Dr. Boville saw to it that schools were soon established in Philadelphia and Chicago, usually in underprivileged areas.

Organization of the National Committee — The number of schools was growing and interest in this new movement was spreading. Some kind of a sponsoring national organization was needed. In 1907 we find . . . Dr. Boville organizing and becoming executive of the National Committee on Daily Vacation Bible Schools. In this he was joined by Judge Alfred P. Seaman and Mr. Russell Colgate. This national Committee numbering 100 had persons on it from 15 cities, eight communions and thirty colleges. Forty-five schools seem to have been held that year, with 140 student teachers.

Schools continued to grow up in many parts of the country. In 1910, sixty cities were maintaining vacation schools, and in 1912, 141 cities. In New York City alone the number of attendants grew from a few thousand to over 30,000. Some of the schools were held in tents set up on vacant lots because there was not adequate space elsewhere. This gave the schools a holiday air and added to their popularity.

Meanwhile, the work was spreading to many cities of Canada. Accordingly, in 1916 the name of the National Committee was changed to International Association of Daily Vacation Bible Schools.

The Denominations Join in Taking Responsibility — A b o u t this time a new development occurred as officials of denominational boards began to realize that this enterprise, which had sprung up spontaneously at about the same time in so many cities, might become an accepted part of the church's philanthropic and educational program. . . . In 1915 it was reported that "denominational boards are taking an interest in the work as a branch of their own activities in mission churches."

.   .   .   .

Meanwhile, the independent and autonomous International Association of Daily Vacation Bible Schools continued to grow and flourish. By 1917 the Association was raising money, borrowing churches, and conducting schools under its own leadership. It developed literature for the vacation Bible schools, it furnished teaching materials and other supplies for them. It sent out teachers as specialists to serve schools in Bible, handcrafts and other subjects.

.   .   .   .

In 1922, the time of the organization of the International Council of Religious Education, the International Association of Daily Vacation Bible Schools became affiliated with the Council.

.   .   .   .

By 1941, 43 countries, other than the United States and Canada, had been enlisted as having had vacation Bible schools.

Present Spread of the Schools — From these modest beginnings this movement has grown to be an enterprise of significant size. Current figures gathered by the Research Services of the International Council, based upon the figures for the year 1949, indicate that there have been received definite reports from 62,161 vacation church schools, which enlisted in that year services of 546,517 officers and teachers, serving a total of 4,045,598 pupils. These figures must be regarded as minimum, for an unknown number of schools are held each year which do not report to any office.

This is an amazing growth for an educational agency, particularly in view of the cataclysmic character of the past fifty years. It indicates that in the vacation church school the churches have found and developed "an idea which has reached its time." Such an idea is one of the strongest things in the world.

The Vacation Church School Belongs to the Present— However glorious the past and its promises for the future, the vacation church school movement must be active, vital, and fruitful in the present to merit a faith in its future. One who carries responsibility for the guidance and promotion of vacation church schools as she works with the various denominational and interdenominational leaders in this field is in a position to speak for the present:[2]

"Today the vacation church school serves well over six million children in more than ninety-five thousand schools. It has been accepted as an integral and vital part of Christian education which can and often does perform a unique function. There are many evidences of its 'coming of age.'

"One of these is the fact that it has been widely accepted as a program worthy of the best possible efforts in leadership training. Many state and city councils of churches, as well as local churches, have developed special programs for the training of vacation church school workers. These special vacation church school training programs also con-

[2] From a member of the staff of the department of children's work for the Division of Christian Education of the National Council of the Churches of Christ in the United States of America.

tribute to the raising of standards for leadership in other parts of the church's program for boys and girls.

"The vacation church school has become widely recognized as an effective means of outreach for the church. Many leaders see a unique evangelistic opportunity in the informal and sometimes community-wide aspects of the vacation church school. They see it as a promising means of bringing unchurched boys and girls into a continuing and vital relationship with the church. In actual practice, however, the evangelistic potential of the vacation church school has only begun to be achieved.

"Another mark of today's vacation church school is its adaptation to the needs of a community in which it finds itself. For example: A church in which mothers find it difficult to give five days a week during the vacation church school may plan the school for Monday, Wednesday, and Friday of several consecutive weeks, thus giving the mother-teachers some time between school days to take care of their housework.

"Today's vacation church school is adapting itself to the needs of varying age groups. For example, junior-high boys and girls often meet in the evening for their classes. The satisfaction that they feel from this respect paid to their grown-upness is evident in their enthusiastic response to the whole program. Such adaptations, seemingly small in themselves, increase significantly the vacation church school's opportunity to serve a variety of situations and needs.

"The vacation church school program of the Christian Church today may be seen as a vast network; one has only to visualize all the local churches and communities represented in the figures cited above. Another expression of this network is the activity of the Committee on Children's Work of the National Council of Churches. This committee now meets once a year and carries on continuous work between times, undergirding the efforts of local church and church council committees. It provides channels of communication through which workers everywhere may share

109

the benefits of their discoveries and experiences with one another. It plans for printed resource materials and in many other ways gives educational guidance.

"This committee has many aspects of children's work as its responsibility, but the importance it attaches to the vacation church school is shown by the large blocks of time given by its members to this part of its responsibility. In these vacation church school efforts the National Council's Junior High Committee is also represented.

"Something of the direction of present-day efforts is suggested in the following purposes toward which the national committee is working:

—to provide the best possible leadership training opportunities for vacation church school workers;

—to reach unchurched boys and girls, as well as those presently enrolled, with effective Christian education;

—to help the church make the vacation church school an integral part of a total summer program, effectively using vacation time for Christian education;

—to help the church make its total summer program an integral and effective part of its whole, round-the-year Christian education program;

—to help churches work with other agencies toward well-rounded and adequate planning for boys and girls within a community.

"Today's vacation church school has much of the same value of the early pioneering adventures. It has a full measure of their potential. Some of the values of the early days, it must be admitted, have been lost; some significant values have been gained, and in many respects significant progress has taken place.

"What has been lost? From the early long-term summer schools, today's typical vacation church school has cut its time down to only two weeks. Perhaps the period can be lengthened again in the future. Furthermore, in all too many cases the vacation church school's outreach to neglected children has been overshadowed by the factors attendant upon fitting it into the established program of the church. The one we should do, not leaving the other undone.

"The other side of the picture, however, shows gratifying progress and maturity when compared with the earlier vacation church school efforts. An outstanding example of such progress is the increasing recognition of the importance of sound educational methods and the continuing effort to incorporate these into all vacation church school programming.

"A minister said to his new director of religious education as she began her responsibilities, 'I am convinced that the vacation church school hasn't scratched the surface yet of what it can do for boys and girls.' This opinion might be disputed, as we count what it has achieved, but it is undoubtedly true when we compare what it has done with what it might do. Never before has the vacation church school been a more ready and sharpened tool waiting for its complete effectiveness only on the kind of use which churches will make of it."

The Vacation Church School Belongs to the Future — As one scans the past history and considers the present picture of the vacation church school, it achieves status beyond expectation of the uninformed. Its services to the church are manifold. While lack of time is a major problem of the church, the vacation church school has led the way into the use of the summertime. It has advanced an informal, socialized, day-by-day program with sufficient time blocks to achieve a reasonable amount of learnings such as are implied in Christian living.

Bearing part of the church's burden of outreach to underprivileged boys and girls and to missionary fields, the vacation church school has also pioneered in co-operating with other churches and with other agencies of the community

111

which are also concerned for boys and girls. One could continue to list achievements and values inherent in the vacation church school movement, but they are stressed over and over again throughout these pages. Let us now look to the future.

Changes are certain when a movement is alive and growing. What are the present signs of change? Are there current trends that given a chance to develop will characterize the vacation church school of tomorrow? Since faith should recognize all the facts and factors and then go beyond them, in the same direction, we may look in faith beyond the present of the vacation church school and in the direction to which current trends are pointing.

A New Look at the Summer — Vacation is associated with the summertime for many people. In the early days, few except school children had vacations. The term vacation for most people meant the days when school was not in session. Now, however, many people have vacations from regular employment. Most of these come in the summer. This has done something to our conception of summer. People expect it to be different from the other nine or ten months of the year.

There have also been changing attitudes concerning the church's use of summer. The summer letdown or summer slump belongs to the past. This does not mean that the churches maintain a high level of attendance through the summer compared to the regular program of the other nine or ten months. It means, rather, a recognition of the unique and fruitful opportunities inherent in the summer—in the vacation mood, in the outdoors, and in the changed pace of activity. Instead of the vacation church school and perhaps the Sunday church school being the only summer activities for boys and girls, the church is coming to regard these as parts of a whole and varied summer program. Planning done for such a summer may be done both by the local church and in co-operation with other community agencies and other churches. (See Chapter 6.)

In many sections of the country the camping program for juniors and junior-high boys and girls is often provided for most of the boys and girls of a local church. How the vacation church school will be related to the camping program may be indicated as follows:

1. The vacation church school and day camping are increasingly related. The vacation church school may initiate projects and interests which are carried on in day-camp experiences once or twice a week for the rest of the summer. Or, this may be reversed when day camping initiates curiosities and interests to be followed up in the vacation church school. In either case a continuity or co-operation of leaders is assumed.

2. Vacation church school goals and camping values are in harmony. Church camping for all ages has made rapid strides over the years. There is not only an increase in number, but the quality of the program has been receiving major attention. Instead of moving the traditional classroom program to the camp as was tried at first, there has now been a program developed which is based on the understanding that boys and girls learn what they live and that camp life offers rich opportunities for Christian living.

Campers live in a simple environment without the confusion and artificiality of much of modern living. They are close to the natural things of God's world. Church camping means living twenty-four hours a day in fellowship with dedicated Christian leaders and with one's fellows. Living together as Christians is given high priority. There are powerful influences toward Christian growth in such an atmosphere where fellowship, work, adventure, and worship yield new insights, perspective, and purpose to life.

Living Together in Christian Ways — There are many manifestations of a developing trend to provide practice in Christian living. This is one of the prior emphases in the camping

113

program. It is increasingly the purpose in church-school teaching. "Thy kingdom come, thy will be done, on earth . . ." not only is a challenge, but surely Jesus thought it was possible. The will of God is more than just a relationship between the individual and God. It is also a relationship with others. Life's greatest adjustments and learnings are many and closely allied. Unless religion helps at this point, civilization will destroy itself.

There are evidences of this change of emphasis in Christian teaching. It is much less concerned with memorization and training in physical and mental skills, but more concerned with the development of persons. This is illustrated in the activity program of the vacation church school. The vacation church school has always emphasized the use of activities as a part of its program. At first these activities stressed manual skills, such as hammock making, woodworking, and sewing because they were fun and baited the interest of boys and girls. Such activities are no longer common. If a hammock was planned as an activity in vacation church school today, the chances are that the group would be concerned for someone who needs a hammock or who would be made happier by receiving it as a gift. The purpose it serves come first. The making of it is secondary. The teacher's first concern is what the boys and girls learn out of such an experience. Teaching that results in the development of persons is the most satisfying kind of teaching, and such development is an essential in Christian community living.

New Requirements for Teachers — It is easier to teach boys and girls to learn to say something than to live it. But the future of Christian education will see an increasing emphasis on living as Christians. This is already evident. Three areas in which we can expect to see development are (1) appreciation for and effective use of group processes, (2) learning to socialize a classroom for more effective Christian living, (3) a growing understanding of the developmental

114

aspect of Christian education. These emphases will require the following study by teachers:

1. *Growing Appreciation for and Effective Use of Group Processes.* What can be new in group experiences since we have been teaching boys and girls in groups through the years? We are finding new significance in group living. It is inherent in Christian fellowship but not always realized. These new studies are being made: the effect of the group on the individual, the opportunities in group life for boys and girls to learn to understand themselves and others, the values in teaching by means of co-operative group action. Many conferences and group studies are centered in these areas. Printed findings are coming out at such a rate as to encourage all of us to restudy the values and dynamic factors in group life so that we may grow as effective group leaders. Many teachers have given little thought to even the simple elements in a group situation, such as may be seen in the following illustration:

Patricia is a dominating person with Susan, a servant to Marilyn, insecure with Carol, lighthearted and creative with Margaret, and is considered an aggressive troublemaker by the group as a whole. A good leader must know that members of a group interact on one another in many ways and seek to understand what each child brings to the group that causes such behavior. Good group experiences should help Patricia, as well as the others, to grow in self-discovery and to grow in co-operative, friendly living. Increasingly in our churches we shall emphasize the need to help leaders develop skill in diagnosing group behavior and in guiding boys and girls in situations through which they mature emotionally and socially as Christians.

Both parents and teachers will need to know that this kind of learning does not take place in isolation for the group contains the dynamic factors which both stimulate and mold such learning. Since teachers and parents are also members of groups in which boys and girls are learning, they will need to become co-operative persons who believe in the goals of Christian social living and have a genuine understanding of how to develop the social consciousness of others.

2. *Learning to Socialize a Classroom for More Effective Christian Living.* Church-school teachers, limited to an hour or two on Sundays, have felt handicapped in socializing a classroom or a group. Even those teachers seeing it happen in the public schools have not fully understood how the church-school teacher and pupils, with limits of time, space, and trained teachers, could enter into co-operative living, working, and achievement. This kind of teaching comes almost naturally to the vacation church school situation. Here is the leisure pace of summertime, and here are blocks of time in which leaders and pupils live together all morning.

Learning to do this has not always been an easy step for many teachers to take. It is not always easy to change from a formal recitation where the teacher is the chief actor, asking questions, hearing answers, and talking, to co-operative work where the teacher is a member of the group as well as consultant and adviser. The socialized classroom will be characterized by group planning, group work, and committee work with reports to one another, pupils taking responsibilities, and the teacher a co-operating member instead of an up-front person. There will be in evidence some plan of organization of the members of the group to assume responsibilities and discharge them, a showing of some independence of thought and action in planning, working, and in evaluating work.

The room will be set up both for group planning and for committee work with working equipment and resources accessible for pupil use. The socialized classroom aims to increase the activity on the part of the pupil as he works, plays, and learns in this business of co-operative living and achievement. Through these experiences the pupil develops a respect for others because of their common interests, purposes, and dependence on one another. Pupils will need to practice independence of thought and of expressing their ideas, but these become subject to evaluation by the group. It is a give-and-take process through which pupils help teach one another, as well as being taught by the teacher.

Evaluation on the part of pupils is essential in this kind of group work. Leaders who help boys and girls to be self-directive are in a position to encourage them to check on their work, attitudes, and behavior. Boys and girls are very free to evaluate the teacher and the teaching. This they always do, and without much mercy. But when boys and girls participate in the planning and work, evaluation has significance. This self-analysis in terms of self-imposed ideals and goals leads to understanding of self and others and becomes a means of both group and personal development.

Such a situation makes new demands on teachers. What kind of person should be sought by the board of Christian education to do such teaching? At least a democratic, co-operative person who is at ease with himself. One who is patient but persistent enough and strong enough to lead a democratic situation where a friendly group spirit develops. Especially one who is willing to learn to teach in new ways. To appreciate the learning and teaching opportunities in all situations is essential.

3. *Growing Understanding of the Developmental Aspect of Christian Education.* Boys and girls are always growing because they are alive. All living things grow. We may nourish or hinder this growth, but growth is a pretty orderly process, and by and large we can assume that certain changes take place within definite age ranges. We count on this development just as do the parents who realize that their boy will wash behind his ears when he develops interest in girls. Abilities develop, too. He could not have washed behind his ears when he was a one-year-old for he lacked physical co-ordination as well as incentive. When the boy was ten, there was no physical disability, but since he is a dynamic, purposive person who finds ear washing both unpleasant and an interruption of what he really wants to do, we say that he has not learned to wash behind his ears.

117

But when the same boy becomes interested in girls he begins to wash behind his ears.

What does this have to do with religious education? We grade because we know that boys and girls have developing abilities and interests; that their developing abilities enable them to respond to an increasing number and complexity of factors, and in an even greater number and variety of ways. It is pretty well understood by experienced teachers that children do not have the same kind of mental processes, attitudes, motives, or desires that adults have. Things look different to a child than to an adult. With added experiences all relationships, events, and actions take on enriched meanings. New ways of doing things and new patterns of behavior develop with the growing person, who from within himself does something with the experiences of life. What he does with these experiences effects subsequent behavior.

If we follow those last statements to their logical conclusion, we realize that a person is learning much that he is not taught for he is the one doing the learning. We need to know the normal and usual course of development so that we can work with a child or youth. We need to know that it is only as the child develops that he is able to experience certain attitudes or to appreciate certain values; that whether or not he is taught, he will be doing something with the stuff of life as he grows and that what he does will determine his future behavior. He is not making mechanical responses to our teaching. He is only making such response as his growth-stage or physical and emotional development, plus what he has done with his previous experiences, allow him to make.

The vacation church school is strategic as the church's opportunity to stress the developmental aspect of Christian education for it does not have to wait a week between sessions nor is it limited to an hour or two a week. Here is the place where boys and girls can be given a chance to be curious and creative, a chance to plan and experiment

118

as they work at their own learning. And this working at their own learning is at the heart of understanding the developmental aspect of growth.

Each generation must adventure in the Christian faith, taking it into the life of its day. It is not enough to try to pass on the Christian heritage, rich and valuable as it is. The Christian faith is something to live out in experience. When Paul knew he was leaving them, he told the Philippians, "In my absence, work out your own salvation with fear and trembling; for God is at work in you" (2:12-13). In much less elegant language a modern teacher said, "There's something cooking inside those children, and I am keeping a fire burning under it." Once a teacher catches a glimpse of the pupil working at his own learning, God at work within, and sees his own part of working with the pupil and with God, he is forever after a different kind of teacher.

The Whole Family Will Be Increasingly Involved — This is a present trend worth watching. The ways in which families may be included in the vacation church school and the attending values have been discussed in preceding chapters. Efforts in this direction have been sporadic and yet persistent. They will continue to persist because of the certainty that unless the home provides a Christian climate for growing life, the church fights against almost impossible odds. An illustration of efforts to involve parents is found in the Cub Scouts. In order to enroll their son, parents have to promise some leadership, perhaps the sponsoring of a den. Many nursery schools and kindergartens follow a similar practice. One of the chief values is the training that the parent receives and the understanding he gets of what the program aims to do for the child. Some Sunday and vacation church schools are now trying this same plan.

The church has hesitated to require parent participation because of its belief that boys and girls have a right to what the church can offer, whether or not their parents are interested. With the growing conviction that what the church does for children needs supplementing by understanding parents, some churches dare to impose a service by parents as a condition for enrollment. This demands skilled leadership in the training of parents, but it adds potential leadership with the boys and girls.

The Vacation Church School and Mass Communication —
There are many places where it is difficult to hold vacation church schools because of distances, transportation problems, and the nature of the working and living conditions. Only the future will tell what use of the radio or television will be employed in carrying the vacation church school into such areas. Being in the lead as a co-operative venture in many communities, using co-operative textbooks, and holding co-operative training institutes, it would not be surprising to find the vacation church school in the lead in the use of television and radio as a mean of giving religious training to boys and girls who for various reasons cannot meet together.

These communication means are used by many agencies for educational purposes. As the various towns and smaller cities add television stations, there are usually opportunities for good educational programs. State and city councils of churches should be alert to both these opportunities and those that come in the multiplying of educational stations. This is an outreach opportunity that needs development and presents a challenge not only to the future church but to the present one.

Experiments in the use of television for purposes of training leaders are already under way by the National Council of Churches in co-operation with city councils. When we can more widely get our training by television and correspondence, we can expect a growing number of prepared leaders. TV and radio can also supplement regular programs for boys and girls.

The future of the vacation church school is in the hands

of those charged with the responsibility of the Christian nurture of boys and girls. The vacation church school movement, itself, is unimportant except as a means to worthy ends. In the past and in the present it has been used to achieve such worthy ends as providing additional teaching time, an effective means of serving the religious needs of boys and girls, a fruitful use of summer, a means of cooperation with other churches and community agencies, an evangelistic outreach in the community, a development of leadership, and an opportunity to learn informal and social methods of group work. Because of such fruitage, the vacation church school has become a recognized member of the total church program. All of this serves as a foundation for whatever use is made of the vacation church school in the future.

Summary — The vacation church school belongs to the past. It has a history with a challenge.

The vacation church school belongs to the present by wide acceptance of special training programs; by adaptation to community needs; by serving a variety of situations; by developing a vast network of interdenominational services; by serving present purposes; by both recognizing the challenge of its history and making present gains.

The vacation church school belongs to the future in trends toward a new look at the summer; a new emphasis on practice in living together as new requirements for teachers and leaders; whole family participation; and possibilities in mass communication.

Suggestions for Things to Do

1. How does the status of vacation church schools compare with the general picture portrayed in this chapter?

2. What gains have been made through the years? What improvements have resulted? What raising of standards has come about? Has there been an increase in numbers?

3. What losses have been sustained? Have the vitality and interest been allowed to drop? Is there an effective outreach beyond the membership?

4. To what extent are the new trends seen in your vacation church school? What solutions to your problems do they suggest?

PART III

PLANNING AND ADMINISTRATION

— 9

Behind the Scenes—

PLANNING

AN INITIATING SPIRIT IS BACK OF EVERY VACATION CHURCH school venture. This initiating spirit may be the board of Christian education, someone of its members, or some other member of the congregation. The minister may be the one who originates the idea and sets it going. He may be the one most concerned if there has never been a vacation church school. His training has helped him know that religious nurture is too weighty an enterprise to be carried by the Sunday church school alone. Sometimes the inititating spirit may be a teacher of boys and girls who feels so desperately the need for more time to do Christian teaching. Or, it may be parents, or any lover of children and youth, who may see the possibilities and start the idea going.

Anyone, therefore, who sees the values in and the need for a vacation church school may be the initiating spirit. What does such a person or group of persons do about it? First of all, they become informed. Much information may be obtained from reading. Denominations promote the vacation church school largely in church magazines and booklets. Councils of churches urge local congregations in their communities to provide vacation church schools for the boys and girls of their neighborhoods. Such councils or federations give guidance and training to encourage these churches and their leaders to do effective planning and work. With promotion, guidance, and the training opportunities provided by denominations and councils of churches, almost any church, even though it is far from urban centers, can find help.

124

Where there is just one or perhaps two persons who have the vision for a vacation church school, it becomes very important to share the enthusiasm with those in position to get something done. The person most interested may not be in position to take the leadership himself, but he can share his enthuisasm with those who should logically take such steps. In some places there is no board of Christian education, and if there is, its members may not have thought about having a vacation church school, may not have the needed vision or information, and it must be admitted that some are disinclined to exert the effort. These conditions are often changed by the enthusiasm of some one individual or group in the church. The power and consequences of one person's enthusiasm cannot be measured. The congregation at large has both the opportunity and responsibility to create a climate in which such an enterprise can be born and come to fruition.

All efforts should tend toward getting the idea of a vacation church school into the flow of general planning. It is conceivable that some one person might have to do most of the planning and carry most of the responsibility for the first year, but even in this situation the efforts will be more lasting if a vacation church school committee is appointed to plan and work along with the enthusiast. A worth-while experience together may result in this group taking future responsibility. This committee should be a part of the group that plans the church's total educational program.

Importance of Early Planning — How many times we hear it said, "It could have been," or, "We might have done this if we had started our planning a little earlier." It is sometimes hard to see the reason for early planning until one is already at work. Many wise leaders have discovered that the best time to begin planning for the next year is before this year's school is over or at least while it is still fresh in mind. Many notes and suggestions could come out of an evaluation of one school that should be kept for use during the year as preparation is made for the next summer's school.

Early planning makes it possible to integrate the vacation church school into the total program of the church (as discussed in Chapter 5). Early planning is essential if the vacation church school is to belong to the community (as discussed in Chapter 6). Early planning makes it possible for the board of Christian education or the official board to provide the funds for the vacation church school in the church budget and to select a vacation church school committee who will serve throughout the year.

The vacation church school committee needs time to select and train workers, to send for and examine books, to plan promotion, and to order equipment and materials for use in the school. After the evaluation of one summer session, the next planning period should not be later than January for the next summer. Many churches find it necessary to meet earlier than this to get the vacation church school in the year's schedule, which is often made by the end of the calendar year. Many denominational and inter-denominational training institutes are held in February, March, and April. Unless local leaders are selected by then, they cannot take advantage of these opportunities.

Organization — The organization for behind-the-scenes planning and work will vary according to the size of the community or church, but the work that needs to be done remains about the same. The organizational pattern on page 127 may be either streamlined or added to, but does suggest the logical people to assume responsibilities.

The Board of Christian Educations Plans — Take a look at the organizational plan of your own local church to see just who is responsible for its educational program. This varies in different denominations and even in local congregations within the denomination. The very smallest church has an official board, and it may do the total Christian education planning for the church. In some denomina-

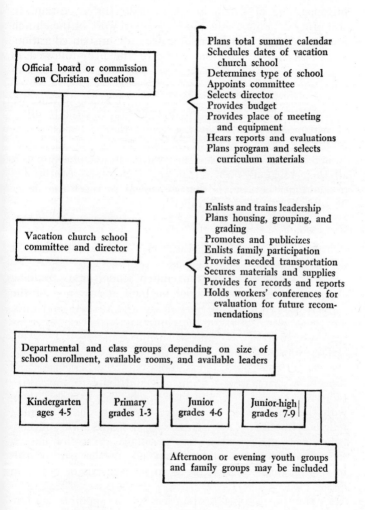

Official board or commission on Christian education

- Plans total summer calendar
- Schedules dates of vacation church school
- Determines type of school
- Appoints committee
- Selects director
- Provides budget
- Provides place of meeting and equipment
- Hears reports and evaluations
- Plans program and selects curriculum materials

Vacation church school committee and director

- Enlists and trains leadership
- Plans housing, grouping, and grading
- Promotes and publicizes
- Enlists family participation
- Provides needed transportation
- Secures materials and supplies
- Provides for records and reports
- Holds workers' conferences for evaluation for future recommendations

Departmental and class groups depending on size of school enrollment, available rooms, and available leaders

| Kindergarten ages 4-5 | Primary grades 1-3 | Junior grades 4-6 | Junior-high grades 7-9 |

Afternoon or evening youth groups and family groups may be included

tions the work of the church is divided into various commissions, one of which is a commission on education. In still other denominations the educational work of the church is delegated to a board or committee on Christian education. Whatever the title of the group or the plan followed in your situation, find out who does the over-all planning in Christian education.

For convenience, and because it is so generally true, we have called this group who makes all the plans the board of Christian education. It is this group that gives wholeness to the educational work of the church. This board is concerned with the total age range within its membership and all their religious needs. It oversees the total educational program of the church that is gauged to meet the needs of all ages within the membership.

Responsibilities— The board of Christian education has certain responsibilities to the vacation church school which it discharges in the following ways:

1. It includes the vacation church school in its thinking about the total church-school program and as one of the various ways of giving Christian nurture to boys and girls. The educational work of the church is carried on in many places, in various ways, and by manifold means.

The Sunday church school, the weekday church school, church camps, youth fellowships, family experiences, and the church service of worship all contribute to the Christian education of boys and girls. Each takes its place along with the others, supplementing, correlating, and deepening religious training. Each has its special significance and contribution to make to Christian growth. The vacation church school is included as a respected and regular part of this total program because it meets so many needs of boys and girls.

2. The board of Christian education appoints a committee and a director to carry on the vacation church school. In some situations the special committee on vaca-

tion church school work is responsible for finding and enlisting the director and other personnel. The committee will be expected to serve throughout the year with responsibilities for planning and carrying out the vacation church school as directed by the board. This means that the board will review the work of this committee, select the director of the school and committee members, act on its recommendations, support it in every possible way, participate in evaluating the school, and plan to relate the values growing out of the vacation church school to the whole church program.

3. The board of Christian education plans for the financial support of the vacation church school. Long-time planning makes it possible to include the cost of the vacation church school in the church budget which is the most satisfactory and unifying way to finance any church-school cost. The whole church assumes more responsibility when the method of financing is a whole church project. In some places the Sunday church school still has its own budget to raise, but the trend is toward a unified church budget with all church-school expenses, whether Sunday, vacation, or weekday, included.

In any case the board of Christian education is responsible for setting up a budget. The amount is usually determined on the recommendation of the vacation church school committee and the director. Many an embarrassment will be avoided if all plans used to finance a vacation church school are approved and guided by this group.

Special gifts may be solicited from other organizations of the church or community; parents may be asked for donations or registration fees; offerings may be taken; but the board of Christian education should consider any such plans from the standpoint of local needs and conditions, always keeping uppermost in their thinking what will best meet the needs of boys and girls. Will asking for donations and registration fees keep some from attending? Would not training in Christian stewardship justify letting boys and

129

girls choose and plan to give their money to others rather than to ask them to contribute to the cost of their own school? It is not recommended to use time while at the vacation church school to prepare a program for adults to see in order to get a good public offering to support the school.

The amount in the budget for a vacation church school differs considerably because so many factors enter into the cost. Some churches have most of the equipment and supplies on hand for just such purposes throughout the year. However, some Sunday church schools regularly use no such supplies, so everything has to be purchased for the vacation church school. The boys and girls may live in the church community, or they may live so far away that the church has to provide transportation.

In some places it may be wise to pay leaders an honorarium to give relief from other responsibility, provide a baby sitter for a teacher's young children, or possibly carfare. Christian laymen and laywomen both give freely of their time and talents, but some who would be very helpful leaders may need to have help in order to give of their services day after day for a period of two to six weeks. All who serve should be supplied with needed books and materials, the cost of which is approved by the vacation church school director and presented to the board of Christian education or its authorized agent.

4. The board of Christian education should plan the total summer calendar scheduling the date and length of the vacation church school and relating it to other summer plans.

The summer becomes important to boys and girls when we think of its possibilities. One week of a vacation church school provides as much time in religious instructions as three months of one-hour Sunday sessions. Multiply this by two to four weeks and see what an opportunity the summer holds. Let the church plan as long a vacation church school as possible!

There is an increasing trend toward relating all summer

activities including, besides the vacation church school, day camps, hobby clubs, story and dramatic clubs, supervised recreation, and church camps for juniors and intermediates. In some areas where the vacation church school is held early in the season some of the summer activities begin there and continue one day a week for the rest of the summer. Family evenings held on the church lawn or in the cool church basement, church family outings, and family camps help strengthen the church and the home.

Let the board of Christian education look at such activities in the light of what they can mean in the religious education of boys and girls and consider including them in a well-planned summer schedule. Let the church be alert to leadership ability among its own members in swimming, baseball, nature hikes, family fun, storytelling, dramatic activities, and other hobbies and crafts. The whole church is enriched by this informal fellowship that the summer makes possible. The vacation church school may be at the heart of it all, giving it emphasis and providing motivation, as well as correlating the summer's activities.

The Time — There are no best dates for the vacation church school except those best for one's own local situation. In the rural area it may be best just after the harvest. In the crowded city, with ten months of public school, it may be best for the churches to co-operate and plan to provide continuous vacation church school opportunities, especially where there are crowded city streets and small apartments offering so little to the young.

Many churches like to begin one week after the public school closes and thereby begin all of the summer activities growing out of vacation church school. In rural areas the time should be selected when families are least busy and can participate as families at suppers, picnics, swims, programs, and special services that may be scheduled for the evening after chores or on Sundays. These extras enrich a vacation church school experience and can deepen the fellowship within the church and its families. The best attendance for vacation church schools for both teachers and pupils will be at times when farm people are between crops or before or after harvest.

In all areas consideration must be given to the best time to obtain the necessary leadership. Avoid the time when leaders are away on vacation in great numbers, or at canning time, if you draw from the mothers who freeze and can vegetables and fruits.

Consider the summer calendar for the community. Try to schedule the vacation church school so that it will not conflict with a "Y" or Scout camp that includes the same people who would otherwise be enrolled. In some places summer-school sessions are held for six weeks following the closing of public school. Some find this the best time to hold a vacation church school for those not in summer school. Others think of it as a conflict so use the time after the public-school summer session closes. Each situation is different, and one must consider all the factors involved. (See Chapter 6.)

So far, we have thought of time as a certain selected portion of the summer. The days of the week and the hours of the day are traditionally Monday through Friday mornings from 8:30 to 11:30 or from 9:00 to 12:00. Any local committee could examine this to see if there is a different schedule for them. Are the distances such that the schedule should be continued from 9:00 A.M. to 4:00 P.M. with special plans made for an adequate rest period, instead of going so many days? In other situations afternoon sessions only are desirable. Others have found that they could lengthen the school term by avoiding Mondays and having four days a week for more weeks. Still others have met most of the summer for two mornings a week with a Wednesday family night comprised of recreation, a movie, and worship.

Age Range — There is a growing trend toward explaining the age range in the vacation church school to include whole families and for making special plans for junior- and senior-high-school groups. One church in an urban community provided light suppers for young people at a low cost per week which were followed by study and planning group worship services, and other activities four evenings a week. The study was related to the regular Youth Fellowship experiences of the church, with most of the services held outdoors in the church yard.

The Director and Vacation Church School Committee Plan — So far, we have thought of the work of the board of Christian education, but many responsibilities will be delegated to the vacation church school committee and the director. They should feel responsible to the board of Christian education as they bring in for approval such recommendations as these:

> the type of school to be held
> the selection of leaders
> the training and preparation of leaders
> the curriculum to be used
> publicity and promotion
> a proposed budget
> reports

The Curriculum — The curriculum is one of the first considerations of the committee because it is a school we are considering and because teaching is a part of it. Unfortunately, there are people who think the vacation church school is an opportune time to ride their hobbies. One woman said, "I always wanted to weave, and we are going to bring someone in to teach weaving to all the girls." A minister said, "I've always used the vacation church school to teach the books of the Bible and to have Bible drills." Both of these things may be done in the vacation church school under certain conditions and with certain age groups, but only when they serve the needs of boys and girls and when they achieve purposes based on those needs.

133

There is something here so deep and vital to Christian growth that it merits some consideration.

Have you wondered why much church-school work has seemed to bear so little fruit? When each new leader comes with personal opinions about the Christian education needs of boys and girls and then with a personal bias determines what should be taught, is it any wonder that teaching is so haphazard, unrelated, and unorganized that it is unfruitful? It is as though a gardener planted a tree on the north side of the house, another gardener decided it should have the southern exposure, a third that it should be pruned close, and a fourth that it should go back to its original setting. The tree would be uprooted and tampered with until its growth would be stunted. A church that wants results in the lives of boys and girls needs a consistent philosophy and policy of Christian education that transcends every phase of the church's program.

She Wanted It in a Box — Let us get rid of another false idea about the vacation church school curriculum. A woman went into a church council's office with a request for a vacation church school program. The director of Christian education asked questions about the local church situation, tried to learn about the ongoing program of the church for the children, and after learning all he could, led the woman to the council's library to see some of the textbooks appropriate for such community schools as the woman represented. The woman spent very little time looking at them, but asked, "Don't you have something that gives the handwork material and the Bible work all in a box so we do not have to have different books for each age?" I have never seen these together "in a box," but I do know that some nondenominational commercial publishing houses try to give an "easy-to-use" package of materials, often nongraded, and unfortunately the theme and materials may overlap the Sunday program or be unfitted to the needs of girls and boys.

Bases of Curriculum Selection— Selection of curriculum material should be made on the basis of the Christian faith and its message and meaning and on the basis of the needs, interests, and experiences of the boys and girls. This will result in grading, for even in a small school of ten pupils the varied needs of older and younger pupils must be considered. There may be particular needs because of the community location and characteristics. A rural church has unusual privileges to appreciate the Creator's world and to co-operate with God in creative work. To utilize this opportunity is the privilege of the rural church.

Another type of community may have special need for learning to live together, especially where boys and girls share crowded playgrounds. It may be that road conditions limit Sunday-school attendance to short sessions of the year, and its boys and girls need those omitted units to study about the Bible, the Church, or missions. In other words, the selection of curriculum should be made in the light of the ongoing experiences of the boys and girls in the Sunday school, home, and community, their previous vacation church school experiences, and a total survey of the units of work used throughout the year. Such a survey can show areas of life left untouched by Christian teaching and help the church avoid overlapping. It is important to see that the total church-school curriculum has balance and progresses toward a realization of all the goals of Christian education.

Another guide in selecting the vacation church school curriculum grows out of the custom many denominations have of agreeing on an emphasis or study theme each year. Because there is so much interdenominational co-operation in the vacation church school program at the local level, in districts, areas, and nationally, there has grown up a plan for rotating the study themes each year for all-around Christian growth and interdenominational use of them the same year. Some of the themes or emphases included in this rotation are:

God and His World
Jesus
The Church
Our Bible Heritage
Personal and Group Relationships
Wider Relationships

When such a plan is generally followed, a child moving from one place to another will not repeat this summer what he had in vacation church school last summer. There is much to be said for following this plan as training institutes can be held interdenominationally that make training available on a theme of interest to all. These institutes are wide-spread across the nation.

Available Texts — When catalogs are examined, a range of textbooks for each age group will be listed for each theme. There are two types of recommended textbooks that have resulted from the denominations working together as well as independently. Working together through the Division of Christian Education of the National Council of Churches the denominations publish co-operative vacation church school texts. Some of the texts are divided into units in such a way that one or more selected units may be used for the shorter school terms. These co-operative vacation church school texts are especially recommended in inter-denominational schools. Many churches working alone also use them. They are based on sound principles and methods commonly accepted with a concern for children.

A second type of vacation church school text is that produced by a denomination for its own use. Many books published by one denomination will have use by other denominations. However, when the theme is on "The Church" or "Wider Relationships," the emphasis may be slanted toward the work of the denomination that published the book.

What makes a good vacation church school textbook? Along with suggested session plans and resources, good textbooks include specific guidance for using materials and meeting the needs of boys and girls. This specific guidance includes suggested schedules, work and study plans, worship suggestions, resources, how and where to find materials and ways of using them, suggestions for activities, and guidance on how to discover and meet the needs of individual boys and girls.

It has often been said that good teachers are helped to grow by using good lesson materials. The vacation church school with its opportunity for longer sessions and a variety of activities provides a good growing climate for teachers eager to grow, so good textbooks should be selected.

In selecting a curriculum theme and textbooks, the committee and director are on the way to determining the program of the school. A good textbook will suggest and give guidance in most of the special features of the vacation church school, including activities, audio-visuals, sharing program, worship, service to others, and field trips and excursions. This guidance does not confine or limit the teacher, but supplements his own resourcefulness in meeting the needs of his boys and girls.

Grouping— When Craig, four, and his sister Christine, six, started for vacation church school, their mother wondered whether she should send Craig. According to the publicity, enrollment was to be from four years to fourteen, but Craig certainly could not profit from the kind of program needed to interest and challenge his six-year-old sister. The mother also knew what would happen if Christine were limited to a program suitable for Craig.

The needs, interests, and capacities are different for children at different ages. The vacation church school that seeks to be most helpful to each boy and girl will group and grade them to make possible the greatest Christian growth and development. As a child grows, there are both constant and changing needs. It is to meet these changing needs that pupils are graded, for while all pupils are different, those of the same age and public-school grade have many interests, needs, and capacities in common.

The usual plan of grouping is as follows:

Kindergarten—four and five years of age
Primary—grades one, two, and three
Junior—grades four, five, and six
Junior high—grades seven, eight, and nine
Senior-high grades are not usually included in most vacation church schools although special provision is often made for them in other ways.

In some situations it might be possible to have classes by grades, in others the two-grade plan, such as grades one and two, three and four, five and six.

Nursery Children and the Vacation Church School — In a recent study it was found that 28 per cent of the vacation church schools reporting to denominational and interdenominational agencies have nursery departments. There have been some unfortunate experiences in which nursery children were taken into the school without adequate preparation for them, even without an understanding of the minimum standards to be observed.

A vacation church school nursery group is often not advisable because of the difficulty of meeting the needs of children this young in a program conducted for two or more hours a day and five days a week. A nursery class should be included only if the following conditions and standards are met to care adequately for this group:

1. Well-qualified, mature leadership for each four to six children and a minimum of two leaders in a group.

2. Enrollment limited to no more than fifteen children per room and who have had their third birthday.

3. Available space of thirty-five square feet of indoor space for each child, good outdoor play space not shared with older boys and girls, and sturdy equipment recommended for a good nursery program.

4. Provision for an informal relaxed schedule with an

opportunity for the children to choose their own activities, have horizontal rest and midmorning juice.

5. Carefully planned introduction of children who may be new to the vacation church school. There may be many children who have not had the opportunity to make a gradual adjustment to the same room and situation and leaders through Sunday-school experiences.

6. Individual and parent-teacher conferences and at least one group meeting in which leaders and parents can think and plan together for the Christian growth of three-year-olds.

Grading — Promotion time in the church school is usually in the fall with boys and girls remaining through the summer in the grades of their last school year. However, there are a number of places where church-school promotion parallels public-school promotion. In such cases the vacation church school sometimes grades on the basis of the next school year. Except for the fact that boys and girls enjoy being in the grade ahead, most teachers would prefer to keep the previous year's grading.

Kindergarten children coming into the primary department lack the experience of regular school work that makes a big difference in their attitudes and abilities to participate with the rest of the primary children. The first-year juniors will not have had experiences with the Bible, that underlies much junior work. If the vacation church school is large enough that each grade meets separately, this is no problem, but many small vacation church schools are organized by departments instead of being closely graded.

On the other side of this problem, some children's workers consider the vacation church school the best place to make the transition from one department to another. The question is usually decided, however, on the basis of promotion time in the local church.

The number of pupils and the place of meeting help determine the number of groups to plan for. Where the number of pupils makes it possible, one teacher may be responsible for the instruction of pupils on one grade level or on one department level which may include two or three grades.

"Do you mean that a teacher must teach his group for the whole two or three hours?" is a frequent question by those just beginning vacation church school teaching. Teachers wonder at first what they can do with a group for so long a time, and then later they wonder how to get it all done in so short a time.

Let us look at some reasons for a group staying together with their leading teacher and whatever associates or helpers this teacher may need. In public schools, lack of adequate preparation of the general elementary-school teacher in special fields led to employment of teachers in various subject areas of the elementary-school curriculum, such as art.

The argument against this plan, causing it to lose force, is the emphasis on integration of experience and on total child development. The Platoon Plan is now one of the less used variations in the elementary school organization. For some time a home-room teacher gave instruction in several subjects, but his pupils would go to the music room, the art room, or the gym for special instruction. Here again instruction in the fundamental subjects was separated from the more socializing experiences of the special rooms and tended to disintegrate rather than integrate the experiences of the child.

Let us look at the self-contained classroom that has been gaining in favor both in public education and in religious education. By self-contained classroom is meant one in which the total program for a group finds direction and unity. The self-contained classroom is led by a teacher who teaches by means of units of work and activities. This teacher, working with the pupils, can more effectively guide the total development of the boy or girl and call in resource people to supplement and assist where specialization is needed in the ongoing work and activity.

140

It is assumed that churches carry on both their Sunday and vacation church school in this way, but unfortunately many have not achieved this ideal. Note the departments of two or three grades that have separate class sessions, but unite for a worship or assembly period under different leaders. If these leaders, usually known as teachers and departmental superintendents, work closely together, the child's experience may still be a "whole" one, but too frequently it means two separate and distinct experiences. Where this pattern exists in Sunday church school, it is often carried over into the vacation church school, but the vacation church school is a good place to learn the better way. For one thing, the space and time problems are less acute, and with enough room and time each group can carry on the variety of experiences needed for good group living and learning.

Housing and Rooms — Imagination and the creative use of space and equipment are the best guarantees of good living and working quarters for the vacation church school. Large, airy rooms are ideal, but even ideal rooms should be used in creative ways that invite boys and girls to work together toward worth-while purposes. Usually the children's own rooms are the best meeting places. Churches that are crowded on Sundays, however, may provide good housing through the week because all the space is available to the boys and girls.

Consider the rooms used by adults or young people who are not in the vacation church school. Are these rooms larger, lighter, and. cooler? Consider porches and yards. Do they increase the space, make more attractive meeting places, and allow enough privacy for good work? Is the regular meeting place for one of the groups a hot room under the roof? Then how about a cool basement in the summer? It is even possible and practical in some places to use homes, private yards, public halls or schools that should always involve a parallel consideration of maintaining good public relations. Where there is no church at all

141

or just a one-room church, it may be necessary to use a tent, a trailer, a store, or some other empty building. In parts of the country that are dry enough the outdoors is frequently used.

The vacation church school committee will be responsible for recommending the best possible meeting places and then when these are approved by the board will make each meeting place clean, livable, attractive, and adapted to good work and living for the boys and girls. Good work is easier when we seek plenty of space, light and air, moveable furniture—chairs and tables the right height for each age—room enough for activities, easy access to the outdoor playground, to water, to toilets, and to materials and supplies with which to work.

In some communities, older children and youth may be invited to come before the opening of the vacation church school to help make the place ready. Teachers will also want time in advance of the opening day to set up their rooms so that they invite interest and activities in the direction of desired achievement. Room arrangements will depend on the nature of the place available, the number of boys and girls, their age range, and the nature of the unit being studied.

A wise teacher clears the room of pictures and other materials used previously and then begins to set it up for the new study. The teacher will ask such questions as, "What pictures and objects will invite and direct the attention and interest to the work activities, and purposes of this unit? What arrangement of furniture will make possible the activities we should be doing in this unit? What centers of interest are needed? Where can we meet together for general planning? How do we create a spot that stimulates quiet and worship?"

What makes a room attractive must be considered from the viewpoint of the boys and girls who are to use it. Maps that would appeal to adults may hold no interest for primary children who are to use the room, while pictures of people and their ways of living would appeal. On the other hand, maps, a globe, pictures, and objects may all appeal to juniors. A room beautifully set up and decorated by teachers may get little response from boys and girls while the opportunity of setting up or decorating a room themselves may end with real pride and at-homeness in the place.

It is said that you can tell a lot about a classroom just by looking, for you can see what it is set up to do. Some classrooms look as though they are set up for the teacher to be an out-front person who does the talking while the pupils sit and listen. Other rooms look as though they would help a teacher with the task, as though the pupils were being invited to and guided in the work, and as though there were real work to do together.

Equipment and Supplies — Good equipment and needed supplies encourage a teacher to try to do good teaching. A teacher is more secure when the conditions help rather than hinder. Many teachers deserve medals for their imagination and efforts in trying to achieve working conditions that make good teaching possible. When we remember that learning comes out of experiences and that boys and girls are active in doing while they learn, we sense the importance of equipment and supplies.

Young children learn by playing and working together. They learn about life by living it. They learn about religion by the interpretation they make through the experiences they are having. They learn about religion by putting it into practice. All of this takes carefully chosen play equipment for work and play centers. Play equipment should be sturdy and the right size for children—not doll size or adult size. Building blocks need to be large enough so that the children can get into what they build. Young children enjoy walking on bridges they make, climbing into a doll bed, and so on. Large play equipment is more essential than little things put on a table to play with.

Primary and older boys and girls also learn through what they do, but their learning differs from that of a younger child. Older children will be making movie reels, creating murals, dramatizing stories, talking with people, planning together, working out programs, writing stories, making maps, worshiping, and in many ways seeking information and sharing with others. Tables and chairs of the right height are essential to good work, and so are the supplies with which the boys and girls work.

Recommended sizes of tables and chairs for various age groups are as follows:

Kindergarten tables, 10-12 inches higher than chair seats, 10-12 inches high.

Primary tables, 10 inches higher than chair seats, 12-14 inches high.

Junior tables, 10 inches higher than chair seats, 15-17 inches high.

Tables may vary in shape. Although rectangular tables have been most popular, some teachers are now using trapezoidal and other shapes that fit best in their space and lend themselves to various uses.

Other equipment needed is as follows:

A supply cupboard, a table to be used for a worship or beauty center, bulletin boards, chalkboards for upper grades, screens or other room dividers if needed, and a piano or record player are all standard pieces of equipment. Pictures, objects, slides, films, records, songs, and books related to the unit being studied should be available. The usual school supplies of pencils, rulers, paper, construction paper, newsprint, cardboard, paints, crayons, clay, paste, paint brushes, scissors, and such items should all be made available as needed and as appropriate to various age groups. It is good to have access to a slide and filmstrip projector and a daylight screen.

In advance of the school some committees gather a supply of cartons of various sizes, string and rope, paper bags, worn sheets that may be dyed, spray painted, or crayoned for hangings, magazines, newspapers, tin cans of various sizes, shelf paper, thumbtacks, clothespins, gummed tape, paper fasteners, a stapler, a first-aid kit, poster cardboard, and wastebaskets. Many textbooks suggest supplies that are to be needed for carrying out the activities proposed in the course being used.

(Standards for proper rooms and equipment are found in *Building and Equipment for Children in the Church*, 195-BC. 25 cents from The Methodist Publishing House.)

Audio-Visuals — Audio-visuals are teaching tools which can enrich the work of a vacation church school in training leaders, in promoting and interpreting a vacation church school to the church and community, in teaching boys and girls, and as resource materials for the use of children as well as their teachers.

Perhaps the best leadership training is found in working with skilled teachers and getting some practice under their guidance. When this is impossible, teachers may see demonstrations of good teaching by means of films. The study suggestions that accompany teaching films and filmstrips usually correlate with leadership education courses and when seriously followed aid in improving teaching.

Does the church need to have a vacation church school interpreted before it is interested or can appreciate the values inherent in such a school? Do members of the board of Christian education, parents, and potential teachers need to be motivated to support such a school? There are slides and filmstrips that interpret the vacation church school in such a way that the church is better able to visualize what it might mean to their boys and girls and how to go about getting ready for it. Many churches take pictures of their school one summer to use the next spring and summer in promotion. Denominational boards of education and councils of churches usually have interpretative and promotional audio-visuals. These can often be seen in vacation church school training conferences.

145

Both projected and nonprojected pictures make good teaching resources. The same standards apply here as to all teaching resources. That is, they should help the ongoing purposes and work of the group. Sometimes a picture leads to worship. It may be used also for instruction to visualize Bible lands, to picture a problem situation or a missionary need. The audio-visuals may be a basis for discussion, may lead to study and service, may introduce or summarize a unit of study, and give interesting information that supplements the ongoing program.

The church that provides a good library of pictures, records, slides, films, and filmstrips will find it valuable to catalogue them so that they may be checked out as study and teaching resources. Just as boys and girls might use a library book, a story, or a picture that fits their need, so they could select a filmstrip to learn about some situation, to visualize a faraway people, and to interpret a condition or problem.

A film may have value in a family night program, too. Perhaps some interpretation may be given in this way concerning the theme of study in the vacation church school. Or, the film might help parents think together about some of the correlating home problems which would be of interest to the whole family. There are also times when families would enjoy a film just for fun. The selection of the film is decided on the basis of its purpose, what it is supposed to do, and how well it will do this for the group seeing it.

Transportation — The vacation church school should be made available to as many children as will attend. Transportation may need to be provided where boys and girls are not within easy walking distance, where there are dangerous traffic crossings, in rural areas, or where the membership may be scattered. There may be unchurched children or those without a vacation church school. These boys and girls could be included in the school of some church willing to provide transportation. Such outreach may be a real missionary service to those outside the church.

Committees may consider such plans as:

1. Renting a bus, providing a reliable driver and another adult to accompany the group, caring for proper insurance, and making a route and schedule. The accompanying adult may be a parent or teacher.

2. Enlisting church members, especially parents, to volunteer the use of their cars and themselves as drivers to transport children of their immediate neighborhoods. Sometimes there are co-operative arrangements in which parents take turns. The church may need to take the initiative in such plans. If the church takes any responsibility in securing drivers and cars, it should be certain that adequate insurance is carried on each car.

3. Providing the gas for leaders' cars and a selected few who are to use their own cars in gathering up the boys and girls on one or more given routes. Teachers usually prefer to arrive ahead of the boys and girls, but in some communities they load their cars with children and thus make greater attendance possible.

4. Advance enrollment cards may have a place for checking one's need for transportation or for volunteering one's service.

Records and Reports— Careful attention to records and reports grows out of our concern for persons. It is strange indeed to see a church school keep strict account of money while neglecting to account for persons. The Christian fellowship and ongoing program of the church are available privileges, but the boys and girls and their parents may need help in becoming vitally interested. Careful records not only help prevent loss of persons to the Christian fellowship but conserve and develop the talents and achievements of people. All records and reports should tell a story. Interpretations should be included when needed for proper evaluation of the progress and achievements of a vacation school.

An enrollment and attendance record may need to show a geographical outreach with percentages from the immediate community or from another area where pupils were transported by bus. Churches usually want to know what percentage of the pupils were from their own membership, from neighboring churches, or from unchurched families. Charts and graphs interpreting statistical data help evaluate the effectiveness of promotion, the opportunity for service to unchurched boys and girls, the wisdom of providing transportation, and the choice of the time and place. Some helpful kinds of records and their uses are indicated in the following charts:

KINDS OF RECORDS	USES OF RECORDS
Individual pupil enrollment records. (Name, address, date of birth, date of enrollment, space for records of progress, achievements, names of parents, their employment and church affiliation)	Used by teachers, pastors, secretaries, parish visitors, to relate pupils to rest of the church program, to enlist home participation, to help with grading and grouping, and understanding each child
Class attendance records	Teachers, secretaries, parish visitors will use such records to urge regularity of attendance. The board of Christian education will use them for evaluations
Leadership personnel records. (Church affiliation, special talents, leadership responsibilities and achievement, with address, telephone number, and training)	Used by board of Christian education as a source of leadership in the total program of the church. Future vacation school committees will use to secure leaders
Financial records and reports. (Itemized sources of finances, itemized cost of school, special offerings by pupils)	Used by board of Christian education as a basis for making next year's budget

148

Public relations records. (Pictures with pertinent data, publicity items, newspaper clippings, announcement posters)	For reports to state councils of Christian education, educational boards of denominations, local church board of Christian education and official board.
Individual growth and interest records	For teachers to note responses, interests, and needs of boys and girls, as a basis for evaluating growth

Summary — Behind the scenes planning includes initiating the vacation church school and organization.

The board of Christian education is concerned with total planning in the church.

Total planning includes the vacation church school and the appointment of the vacation church school committee and director.

The director and vacation church school committee are responsible to the board of Christian education for recommendations, reports, curriculum selection, grouping and grading, schedules and classrooms, equipment, supplies, transportation, records, and reports.

Suggestions for Things to Do

1. Success is not easily measured for it springs from unseen planning. Neither does one measure progress unless the beginning place is known. This is not always easy to ascertain, but it is important for you to find the beginning place in your local church. Where do you start? Is some organizational work needed? What new committees need to be appointed?

2. Make a schedule of long-range plans needed in your local church indicating month by month what planning must be done.

3. Order guidance materials from your own denominational board.

4. Find out what training programs are available.

10

Leadership Is the Key—

DISCOVERING AND ENLISTING

WHILE LEADERSHIP IS THE KEY THAT UNLOCKS THE SUCCESSFUL vacation church school, it is also a problem. Lack of leaders eliminates many vacation church schools. This most important factor in planning must be dealt with realistically, humbly, and positively. There is no use in making glowing statements about what ought to be done unless one has practically and realistically met such problems and can give guidance born out of the successful experiences of many people.

We should face the fact that there is no magic formula for providing leaders. Neither is hard work alone enough. Some have worked diligently, over long periods of time, trying to enlist leaders, and are still faced with inadequate staffs in their church schools. It is futile for an administrator to blame his predecessors of ten and twenty years ago because they did not inaugurate a systematic plan for producing leaders for the church, but we can begin now to provide leaders. Even though the present may not be all it ought to be, it should at least be one of growing promise and fulfillment.

Fruitful ways of facing our leadership problems are:

1. Know what vacation church school leaders are needed, their duties and qualifications. (High-school students should not have responsibility for teaching a group all alone. In some cases they might serve as helping teachers.)

2. Work in the faith that there are people in every church who care about the religious growth and development of boys and girls.

3. Learn about tested ways of discovering, enlisting, and training such persons for leadership in the local church.

4. Begin now a systematic plan of leadership discovery, enlistment, and training that will bear fruit this year and for the years to come.

Before discussing these four phases of solving our leadership problems, a word should be said about the spirit in which such a task is undertaken. It is assumed that those who read this book are looking for help and are dedicated to the service of boys and girls. Dedication of time and energy as co-workers with God is also assumed. This means to believe and act as though God is our source of motivation and power and that achievement comes as we work with his purposes.

Many Christian leaders have this faith. With some it is only passive, but it needs to be actively demonstrated and proved. Many of us forget what our part of the partnership with God entails. We know it includes doing our part of the work. We should also know it includes a certain quality of spirit that is contagious. "A cheerful heart is a good medicine." (Proverbs 17:22.) This is the kind of medicine needed by sick churches. Enthusiasm and cheerful, optimistic faith are contagious. The doleful, doubtful, pessimistic administrator will never achieve what the contagiously enthusiastic man of God produces. When our faith and enthusiasm are coupled with good hard work, we shall be amazed at the results. This attitude and practice are religiously sound and fruitful.

Vacation Church School Leaders — *The minister* has a vital role in the vacation church school. If he understands the needs of boys and girls and sees the possibilities in the vacation school to meet those needs, he may initiate the whole idea in his church. He may be the one to create interest and enlist the support of the church. He may even have to carry the responsibility of such a school until he can demonstrate its values, perhaps serving as its director.

151

When the minister does carry this responsibility, he should cultivate and enlist those who should logically be responsible for organization and administrative duties. When the minister has an active and responsible committee and director at work, he still should know what makes a good vacation church school in practice and organization and be able to evaluate the plans and results. In other words, he is interested in and supports the vacation church school just as he does all that serves the needs of his people.

The Role of the Minister — The following testimony of a minister indicates something of his role:[1]

"The vacation church school offers the minister his most promising opportunity for setting the tone and determining the effectiveness of the Christian education program in his church. In the small church, in all probability, the minister must give direct and vital leadership in organization and in teaching. He plans with what class teachers and superintendents he has. The minister's sense of values concerning the importance and function of the vacation church school can be shared with these leading persons, and together they can develop a teaching staff.

"I have had my best success in assembling a staff when I was able to make the call and take the approved texts to the prospective teacher. In the call it was possible to explain what we were trying to accomplish in the school, our philosophy of teaching through activities of work, worship, fellowship, and study. This kind of personal contact permits the minister to impart his feeling about the importance, the opportunity, and the breadth of method of the vacation church school. Special training groups may be set up to study specific plans and how to carry them out.

"In the actual operation of the school a minister works wherever he can be most effective, usually wherever the greatest need exists.

---

[1] Reported by the Reverend John Tennant, First Methodist Church, Albion, Michigan.

"Working thus directly with the boys and girls and in staff conferences with teachers as well as in consultation with department heads, the minister can establish warm personal relations with children and their leaders. He is thus recognized as one who is accessible, informed, and able not only in corporate worship on Sunday morning but in the program of Christian education in the church. His participation in that program builds morale within and among his teachers and leaders. The wise minister will not monopolize leadership, but will use these opportunities for the creation of a self-propelled core of departmental leaders and a knowing and understanding group of church-school teachers.

"In the larger church it is frequently possible to find department leaders who are capable of securing vacation church school personnel and who are altogether capable of organizing interdepartmental co-ordination. Some are able to do more effective teaching than the minister. In such cases the minister is most helpful in getting frequent preliminary conferences for planning with these leaders. The minister guides all leaders in using proper materials, making advance preparation, and in seeing that the total planning for the school meets the highest possible standards.

"Even in a well-staffed vacation church school the minister may quietly and courteously ask for an opportunity to serve in some position in order to come to know the boys and girls and so that they may come to know and identify him as one who is interested in them and the church school. This interest is more difficult to demonstrate in the normal church year.

"The minister must work carefully so as not to destroy or belittle exiting leadership. Nevertheless, he does carry responsibility for the total program of Christian education in his parish and therefore must serve with the board of Christian education and chosen officials in selecting and securing personnel, and certainly in supporting the vacation church school by his regular presence during its period of operation. As the years of association pass in one parish, it should be less and less necessary for the minister to direct and more and more possible for him to turn to the role of encourager even when he makes suggestions for improvement.

"One of my most valuable experiences was to lead a high-school group that assembled for one hour of instruction each morning. For the remaining hour and a half these high-school people worked in several departments as helpers. They assisted in activities, played the piano, prepared and served a lunch for the kindergarten children, and helped clean classrooms before, after, and during sessions.

"Through such training and service the high-school young people got the feel of Christian teaching, and many came to anticipate future service as church-school teachers. In several churches I was able to see youngsters who had begun in the high-school department of the vacation church school later joyously working as teacher in the Sunday church school. I believe that they were teaching because of the attitudes they learned and the experiences they had while themselves high-school pupils in these vacation church schools."

The Director and the Vacation Church School Committee — When a suburban church was looking for a director, they found him in Mr. Frank, who was a high-school principal. Mr. Frank was a good administrator and organizer. He knew how to get people to work and how to delegate responsibility. With Mr. Frank in mind as director, the board of Christian education knew that one of the committee members should be a person who knew and understood children and who understood what a vacation church school could mean to boys and girls. This person would have contacts in the children's division of the Sunday school, preferably be an active worker there. It turned out that this person became the supervisor of the school who helped the teachers plan their work.

Another member of the committee was one who had experience in public relations and who took the responsibility for publicity and promotion. A third member of the committee was Mr. Marsh, a retired man, who had lots of time on his hands and enjoyed getting materials and equipment which the supervisor and teachers requested. Their teaching work was lighter and more effective because Mr. Marsh had time, not only to order and get supplies, but to be on hand to distribute them, and in an emergency to get some unforeseen piece of needed equipment. A fourth member of the vacation church school committee was a member of the church's recreation committee. The correlation between these two groups through this man resulted in a continuation of certain constructive activities through the rest of the summer after the vacation church school was supposedly over.

The Director's Duties — As a rule the director is the key person who actually serves as a principal or supervisor directly in charge of the school. The director needs to be experienced and trained, one who can understand the needs of boys and girls, guide the selection of curriculum, work with the teachers and parents, help to group and grade the school and unify all its working parts on a high educational level of Christian teaching. Such a person should be able to work well with both adults and children, should know the church and community resources, should be directly in charge of the organization and administration of the school, and should be in close touch with the church's total educational program.

In the preceding story, Mr. Frank did not do all of this himself. He was able to delegate certain tasks to the committee selected to work with him. In fact, the committee members were chosen because they could serve in this way. The actual supervision of teaching through joint planning and helping teachers prepare to teach was delegated to another person, called a supervisor.

155

Sometimes the director is chosen because of the ability to combine the duties of director and supervisor as in the case of a smaller church where Mrs. Lee seemed to be the logical person both to direct and to supervise the school. She was called the director of the vacation church school.

Mrs. Lee was the children's division superintendent of the Sunday school. First of all, she was used to working with the teachers and department superintendents. She dreamed about what could be done for boys and girls if there was more time, and she knew how to relate the work of the Sunday and the vacation church schools. Mrs. Lee also knew how to enlist the assistance of others who were active in the Sunday church school. While it was not her responsibility to get all the leaders, Mrs. Lee did have the enthusiasm that was contagious, and she knew some qualified persons who were able to work on weekday mornings in the summer. Mrs. Lee's outstanding quality was her ability to work with people and to supervise the school. She understood boys and girls and knew how to plan a school that would guide them in Christian learning and living. She could help teachers plan their work; she could correlate various phases of the program and keep it all on a high level.

Whether the same person serves as both director and supervisor depends on the local situation and the qualifications of the people involved. At any rate when selecting the whole committee seek the variety of qualifications needed to plan, conduct, and supervise an effective vacation church school.

Teachers and Assistants — The preferred teachers for most vacation church schools are the regular church-school teachers of the boys and girls. The added time together can deepen the teacher's insight into the needs and interests of the pupils and can strengthen the bond of fellowship and understanding between teacher and pupil. Interests developed through the church-school year may be consummated in a vacation church school program with its more generous time schedule. And conversely, interests developed in the vacation church school may be further pursued and related to the ongoing work of the Sunday school. Realizing that regular teachers are not always available, and that there may be just as good and sometimes even better teachers who can serve on weekdays in summer, let us consider qualifications to look for in teachers and associate teachers.

Teacher Qualifications — Every teacher should be a practicing Christian. We should not expect every person to express himself in the same way, but a teacher needs a faith that is revealed in his daily living.

A teacher needs to be a mature person. Assistants may be chosen from the older high-school and older youth groups provided adequate training and supervision are given, but the person in charge of each group should be adult, should understand the boys and girls of the age which he attempts to teach, and should have some experience in group work.

A highly desirable qualification is the willingness to learn to be a good teacher. The person who expects to teach as he has always taught, or as he was taught when he was young, and who refuses to read, take training, or profit from the workers' conferences is a good person to avoid. A willingness to learn and to adventure in new ways of teaching, to grow, and to change are often more desirable than experience if one cannot find both. The willingness to learn to be a good teacher includes being willing to prepare carefully for each teaching session. We ask very busy people to be teachers in our church schools, but we should never give them the impression that we can use them as teachers if they cannot or will not find the time to make adequate preparation. Those who are really interested will find time to do what they consider important.

A teacher, as well as all other vacation church school leaders, should be co-operative. Appreciation of the contributions of others and of the richness of experience for boys and girls that comes from various people is basic to a co-operative spirit. Teachers have to work with others—parents, other teachers, supervisors, director, and the vacation church school committee. In the family of Christian workers co-operation is an essential qualification.

Assistants and helpers are needed when groups are large. For example, a kindergarten teacher alone should not have more than five to eight children. An assistant or additional teacher is required for each additional five to eight children. Assistants should have the potential qualifications of a regular teacher. They should be able to follow the lead of an experienced teacher, supporting his plans and purposes. All assistants should be mature enough to assume responsibilities for the care of children and to seek counseling from the more experienced person. This means that junior-high boys and girls should not be recruited as assistants.

Being Democratic and Having Discipline — As one discovers the values in group planning and living, he becomes aware that teachers and other workers need to be democratic in all relationships with boys and girls. This includes being sensitive to the needs of boys and girls so that they feel wanted, find tasks in which they feel useful, and increasingly assume inner control. Security and personal recognition of their achievements are needed by boys and girls if they are to set up purposes toward which they will work. A friendly, permissive group relationship must exist for the pupils who achieve self-control. Some adults know only how to direct rather than stimulate and guide boys and girls to make choices, decisions, and evaluations.

Much of what we know as discipline is now thought of as accepted self-control in which there is freedom to make group choices, to understand and appraise group progress and behavior, and to be guided by group approval. These new ways of discipline are dependent on the ability of teachers to adapt the ways of the classroom or school to the pupil while they themselves are disciplined, understanding, and democratic persons. This closer relationship between teacher and pupil also demands more of the teacher in sense of purpose and direction, resourcefulness, and a belief in the democratic process.

When Miss Coleman was teaching the primary children, she prided herself on order and discipline. True enough, there did seem to be order, for as her pupils left the room, they all came out two by two. The supervisor became suspicious of the kind of order and discipline in which, when the children reached the outside door, they burst into boisterous pushing and yelling. A visit to Miss Coleman's room revealed Miss Coleman saying such things as, "Now we shall all make a frieze." "Now we shall put away our work." "Now we shall have a story." In other words, all the plans and decisions were made by Miss Coleman, who told the children just what to do and how and when. After she had worked for a few days with the supervisor, one could notice a gradual change in Miss Coleman and might hear these statements instead: "Could we show this better in a frieze or a display?" "Let's plan our time together." "We could use either paints or crayons; which do you choose?" "When the committees finish their tasks, we will have used the time."

Miss Coleman had to become more flexible, it is true, and had to depend more on the children's choices for what went on in her classroom, but when she did this, she found that she could also help the boys and girls grow and change through evaluating their workmanship. They then considered together such questions as, "How well did we do in making our frieze?" "How can we improve our next piece of work?" "What caused our frieze to break in the middle?"

In finding and selecting teachers for the vacation church school it is important to keep in mind these elements that make for democratic group living. The teacher does not just turn over everything to the pupils but does seek to help them develop ability to set goals, to plan work, to make choices, and to criticize themselves as they grow in understanding of one another and in how to consider the welfare of the group.

Democratic Christian living assumes the desire and ability to live harmoniously with one another and for the best interest of all. But in order to achieve this high level of living one must always develop inner controls based on concern for others. We cannot expect boys and girls to have any sound basis for evaluating their actions unless they have a real part in the continuous planning of their experiences. If it has all been teacher directed, how can the boys and girls be held responsible for either their work or their behavior? In selecting teachers let us try to discover those who are willing to adventure in these new ways of teaching.

Resource People— Because our minds are so set in the traditional teacher pattern, many resources for leadership are going to waste. Among the members of a church or the people of a community are persons of varying talents, interests, and experiences whose contributions to a group can make the difference between boredom and exciting interest. As illustrations of how resource leaders may be used consider the following incidents which I have noted:

The junior highs of a small town were studying "Christians Around the World" and were making a large book of clippings and pictures interpreting world events of significance. The bishop of the area, with his wife, came to the town for one Sunday. They had recently made a trip around the world so the junior highs made up a list of questions and invited the bishop's wife to discuss these questions with them in the light of her recent experiences.

One junior group studying "Palestine in Jesus' Day" asked a junior-high teacher who had served two summers as a counselor in a Jewish camp to explain some of the Jewish religious customs. She met with one committee of the

160

juniors for an hour each day for a week as they developed a play built around Jewish religious customs. A Bible professor who lived in the town spent one hour helping them experience the way the boys might have studied Hebrew in the synagogue school.

A primary group was busy in a unit on "The Church." They had a half hour with the minister, and interviewed the sexton and organist.

A minister who loved to sing helped his primary children create their own music for two verses of Psalms 100. He came to the session three different days as the children worked on this.

Another group of juniors studying "How People Make Their Work Christian" found several people about town to interview: a veterinarian, a writer, a nurse, a blind mathematics teacher, and a returned missionary.

In all of these incidents the experiences of the boys and girls were enriched by the wise use of outside resource people. This is only a hint of the unnumbered possibilities to be found in both rural and urban centers. A few guiding principles should be observed when resource persons are used:

1. The regular teacher and his class keep planning and working toward their goals. Resource people are brought in because they help reach these goals. The ways in which a group reaches its goals may be different because of the available resources, but available resources should not deflect from accepted purposes.

2. Resource people should be interviewed by the teacher in advance in order to have the purposes understood by the resource person and so the resource person would know how he fits into the whole picture as well as the amount of time available to him.

Other Helpers — Other helpers needed vary with the size and place of the vacation church school. Secretarial help relieves teachers of many details, such as keeping records and

161

making reports. A secretary really interested in boys and girls and in their attendance can make them feel welcome and at home as they arrive. Imagine the helpful secretary who called each absentee during the first hour. In that school there was almost perfect attendance. Other secretaries give teachers a list of their absentees as soon as the group has gathered.

The caretaker or custodian should both give and receive co-operation. He should be considered as a member of the staff of workers so that through joint planning teamwork results.

When boys and girls clean up after themselves and learn to return materials to their proper place, they are both practicing good group behavior and developing appreciation for the custodian, for cleanliness, and for the property of the church.

Recreation Leaders — Play serves many purposes. Recreation leaders find it a means of better understanding their boys and girls. The relaxed atmosphere of a playground helps boys and girls to be more at ease with themselves and with other members of the group. Play may satisfy fellowship needs, give wholesome emotional release, and satisfy physical needs.

When groups are informally active in much of their group work, the need for hard physical exercise during a morning is not as acute. On the other hand, teachers should be increasingly sensitive to the emotional and physical needs of boys and girls and ready to introduce active play when it is needed. Many consider the advantages found in playing with the boys and girls justify the efforts made. This makes special recreation leaders less regularly needed.

On the other hand, playground leaders can assist by organizing and guiding playground activities especially if they seek to co-operate with the teachers who are working toward certain purposes through play. All playground leaders should hold a high standard of Christian living as the playground becomes a place in which boys and girls may learn to practice Christian principles and relationships. The therapeutic values in play should be understood by all play leaders.

Music Assistants — Every teacher wishes he could lead his own group in singing, and to a great extent he does determine what music is selected and how it is used, whether for listening, singing, recreation, or worship. Music has many values that contribute to the purposes to be achieved so one does not just turn the music over to a resource person. Rather, the music helpers and teachers confer.

A nationally known musician visited in a village when the vacation church school was in session. She was asked to spend a period with the junior-high group. This experienced music leader knew the power of music to achieve ongoing purposes and had three conferences with the teacher in preparation for leading that half hour of music. No wonder she took this group from where it was to where it should be going! And if she, so experienced and trained, needed this kind of co-operative preparation, what about other musicians, either singers or pianists, who are to serve boys and girls? Common understanding of purposes and procedures results from co-operative planning and is good practice among all vacation church school leaders.

Discovering and Enlisting Leaders Through the Pulpit—Every church has sincere and earnest Christians in its membership. These kinds of persons care about the religious nurture of boys and girls. Not all Christians make good teachers, but many sincere and earnest Christians can be enlisted in the concern for leadership. Jesus' admonition to pray the Lord of the harvest to send forth laborers is a good precedent. It is also important for the church membership to be kept informed and to have an intelligent concern.

The pulpit is one medium through which the adult membership of the church could be informed about the purposes of Christian nurture to meet the needs of boys and girls. Unfortunately, those churches most in need of leaders receive the least guidance, and their adult members are most illiterate about the needs for and demands of Christian education. Ministers are in a peculiarly significant position to lead their congregations to an intelligent and motivating concern for the Christian nurture of children and youth. Some present the needs for service in their sermons and follow with a commitment service where members are given opportunity to indicate their form of service, talents, and abilities so that the service file of the church continues to supply potential leaders. Ministers who share with their congregations the need for and value of serving in the educational program of the church will have a people with more intelligent concern and greater willingness to serve. But specific invitations should be given personally to all prospects hand-picked for particular jobs.

A Personnel Committee — While the whole church membership should be solicitous for discovering leaders and should be concerned for the needed qualifications, there should be several carefully selected people who will compose a personnel committee under the direction of the board of Christian education. The minister, the director of Christian education (if there is one), the church-school superintendent, and the divisional superintendents are all logical people to serve on such a committee. But we must remember that all of these persons have other responsibilities that are neglected if they have to bear the burden of discovering and enlisting new leaders. Consequently, some churches have entirely separate persons serving on the personnel committee.

One church in Michigan has on its committee the personnel director of a large manufacturing company who also knows the membership of the church quite well; a businessman who is very familiar with the church's program and a long-time resident who knows the people, an active Woman's Society member, the minister, and the superintendent of the church school. The board of Christian education places before this committee quarterly a list of needed leaders: secretaries, teachers, associate teachers, youth counselors, or whoever is needed. The director of the vacation church school should work with such a committee where there is one. The personnel committee should have on its list those persons who could serve for a few weeks each summer— students, housewives, and public-school teachers. It may be that the personnel committee has a list of resource people who do special things well, such as leading music or choral reading, making maps or costumes, making phone calls, or driving cars. The personnel committee should study carefully the job analysis for each leader to be enlisted.

The Regular Church School Leaders — The first place to seek vacation church school leadership is from those already teaching the same boys and girls in the Sunday church school so that the various parts of the church school provide a wholeness of experience rather than separate and unrelated experiences. Perhaps at least one teacher in each group may be a Sunday church-school teacher. This is important for continuity. But it is well also to have new recruits on the staff. Projects desired but otherwise set aside for lack of time may then be undertaken because the same group with continuing leadership has more time. Another rewarding value of teaching one's regular pupils in a vacation church school is a new understanding of them. Four regular junior teachers of one church who just completed a vacation church school with their juniors were overheard to say: "I did not know these youngsters could get so interested. That must be because they had a chance really to do something. They worked so hard! They came early and stayed late. After I planned with them, they just took over. I feel that I know them so much better. I also think I know better how to teach them. From now on I am going to rearrange my room and change my whole way of teaching."

These are rather startling conclusions to come from one vacation church school term. In what other way could the regular church-school leaders have achieved this new outlook on their pupils and on the way of teaching them?

A junior-high teacher spent a week of his vacation in the vacation church school to be with his boys and girls. He reported to his pastor, "When I saw what that group could do, I knew I had been trying to do too much for them. No wonder they got bored with so much talk from me. That must be the reason the church loses so many boys and girls of this age. From now on I am letting them work, and I believe they are going to like it enough to stick with us." The pastor reported that the prediction was right; it was a changed department with gains rather than losses.

Teaching in the vacation church school can be good training in better ways of teaching. It gives motivation for continuing training and growth on the part of the experienced workers. The training institutes and vacation church school clinics that are provided, the vacation church school textbooks guiding toward more active ways of learning, and the more relaxed and increased time schedule all combine to improve teaching and teachers.

Teaching Potential in the Congregation— The p e r s o n n e l committee of a large church met to find additional leaders for the church school. They realized that their list of prospective leaders was inadequate to supply their needs. They took the membership roll and considered the leadership possibilities of each person listed there, and then they made up a new list. The following will illustrate:

> Adams, J. A.—a hardware merchant about fifty; knows the whole town; likes detail work; would make a good treasurer.
> Allen, Mrs. Mary—public-school principal about forty; successful with children; has home responsibilities so time is limited; could serve the church best on its library committee.

Barry, Felix—Twenty-two and home from college this summer; has some playground experience; especially popular with junior-high boys; possibility for summer playground leader.

Bascom, Alice—nineteen, secretary, active in youth society during high school; served as secretary in primary department; would make a good primary church-school teacher.

By the time the committee went through the membership roll, there was a new list of prospective church-school workers. Enlistment in training would be the next step.

How to Enlist Leaders — The following suggestions include those given previously in this chapter but which are here summarized:

1. A cheerful and contagious enthusiasm on the part of the recruiter with a radiant Christian faith and confidence.

2. An informed congregation challenged from the pulpit and in various church groups by lay persons who administer the church's program.

3. Personal enlistment of selected people confronted by a personnel committee (or others charged with the responsibility of enlisting leaders) to accept leadership duties which are to be preceded by training to do effective work.

4. A great enough challenge and allotted time to make preparation so that leadership will be taken seriously. Avoid last-minute enlistment asking for help tomorrow or next week. Set a time schedule, such as a January deadline, to secure summer leadership or a May deadline for securing leaders to begin the new church-school year in October. Extras may be enlisted for emergency losses. While this sounds ideal, it is a practical and successfully tried plan that generates a lot of satisfaction to its users.

5. Develop a fellowship among groups of workers that is rich enough and dynamic enough to attract others. This fellowship will consist of planning together, experimenting together, working together, and taking training.

6. Instead of getting along with a minimum of leadership, enlarge the staff of workers. It is much easier to get two people to teach a class than just one. Suppose Mrs. Baker would make a good kindergarten teacher. The one who goes to enlist Mrs. Baker might say to her, "Mrs. Baker, our committee is aware that you have certain qualifications (naming them) that are needed in a kindergarten teacher. We have a group of twelve four-year-olds for which we shall need a teacher next summer. Even with all of your qualifications we do not want to ask you to take on this responsibility alone, for a teacher needs to keep in touch with each child's home and to learn the child's interests and needs. You would be less burdened and also be able to do better teaching if someone shares the responsibility with you. Before we ask for your decision, we would like to ask you if there is someone in the church with whom you would especially like to be associated and to have us secure as your associate teacher."

Some such approach as this makes it possible for Mrs. Baker to realize that she does not have to be responsible for the whole load alone and that she may help select a worker congenial to her. It also gives the personnel committee a good lead to another possible worker and a persuasive appeal: "Mrs. Baker has asked for you." Out of much experience with this plan one can now be assured of its values, one of which is that it is easier to get two people than one for such a task, and another, that it encourages a higher quality of work. The plan assumes that people will need to be guided in how to work together. It is never good to take turnabout being the leader.

On the other hand, two people may share alike in working with a group. Or the responsibilities may be divided so that each knows for what he is responsible. Planning together is essential. It is also essential that the distinction be kept clear between an assistant (or helper) and an associate. An associate has equal status. When the people work together, they should not be made to work according to the same pattern of any other two teachers. Each team should be helped to work out its own pattern of co-operation.

11

Leadership Is the Key—

TRAINING AND SUPERVISION

TRAINING LEADERS FOR VACATION CHURCH SCHOOL SHOULD be a continuous practice in the local church. New groups of leaders are constantly needed to replace those who move away or for other reasons have resigned. Even the smallest church needs to keep an incoming group getting ready to teach, to do secretarial work, and to serve as superintendents or counselors. Even the smallest church can keep up-to-date manuals and books to read and can give some training through association of potential leaders with those who are most experienced. A church that prepares for its year-round program in this way is already preparing for its vacation church school leadership needs.

Read and Study Together — What else can the local church do to prepare leaders for the vacation church school? If the leaders are enlisted in the winter with four to six months to get ready, their reading may be guided to manuals and books helping to interpret the purposes of the vacation church school and how to conduct one. Teachers may have their textbooks long in advance to be getting acquainted with them. As they read and study their textbooks, they will begin to be aware of materials that can be put aside for use—pictures in magazines, clippings for the browsing table or bulletin board, cardboard tubes from rolls of paper for which there will be special use, a picture book found when browsing in the bookstore.

A vacation church school teachers' meeting, long in advance of the school, stimulates teachers to study and plan together. They may have practice sessions in which they may make a diorama as suggested in the text. What if no one has ever used this activity before? The textbook tells how, and doing it together gives the teachers both a new skill and a fellowship with others while learning.

Audio-Visuals—See How It Is Done — The multiplying number of helpful audio-visuals makes it possible to go beyond reading to see and hear how others teach or conduct a vacation church school. One also can make a special study of the age group to be taught through studying films and filmstrips. While reading can be very helpful in thinking through the meaning of teaching, many teachers need to see in order fully to comprehend how one uses the Bible with a group, how to lead a discussion in which the leader is one of the group, how to do committee work, how to teach a new song, or how to guide the play interests of children. When using audio-visuals make them a subject of study and discussion rather than just something to see and forget.

Any one church can use audio-visuals, and the farther the church is from other training centers, the more important it is to make this kind of training available to one's workers. Community, county, and state institutes and leadership schools for vacation church school workers will also use audio-visuals. If all the workers of a local church can attend these larger groups, it is not as necessary for the local church to rent so much in the way of training films and filmstrips, and the cost for using audio-visuals is considerably lessened when large groups get together. Denominational area offices and state, city, and county councils of churches often make training filmstrips available at little or no cost.

Institutes, Workshops, Skill Shops, Laboratory Schools, and Leadership School Courses — Outside the local church there are many training opportunities. Urban centers in every part

170

of the United States provide some means of preparing and training vacation church school teachers and leaders. Many county and rural areas are also covered by vacation church school institutes within driving distances. While groups of churches within one denomination may associate for this purpose, there is widespread interdenominational practice in training vacation church school leadership.

The fact that many denominations now unite interdenominationally on a theme for the year makes it possible for the training to be specifically practical. For instance, primary workers can meet together and study their textbooks and stimulate and help one another with usable suggestions. Directors and supervisors can plan ways of coordinating the whole school. Schools within a community can plan to share resources, such as enlisting the public library's interest in making displays, and reserving books, films, or pictures on the theme of the year. Some community projects may be undertaken jointly by several vacation church schools. Suggestions for this kind of community-wide interest often come from the special training institute or school.

The Supervision of Teaching — Who supervises the teaching in a vacation church school? It may be the minister who is best qualified to help teachers. When he helps them in advance preparation, with teaching problems along the way and to improve their teaching, the minister is supervising whether or not he assumes this title. Or, the supervision may be done by the director of the vacation church school. In large vacation church schools where there are superintendents of departments, they may be the ones to supervise the teachers of their grades. Sometimes public-school teachers with religious education background can be enlisted for supervision.

The first task of a supervisor is to help teachers do the best teaching of which they are capable. Supervisors are better understood as helpers and encouragers rather than

171

critics. Only so will teachers seek supervision. A qualified and understanding supervisor will give teachers a sense of security, encouragement, support, and a desire to improve their teaching.

More specifically, the tasks of a supervisor working with teachers may be to:

1. Make available the best teaching materials. Have them ready and at hand for the teacher's use.

2. Provide teaching resources or give explicit guidance as to where and how they may be obtained with some indication of their use and values.

3. Guide teachers in preparing to teach by helping them better understand their pupils, plan their teaching procedures, prepare their rooms, and develop any needed skills for leading pupils in planning or in activities.

4. Provide the best training opportunities possible through reading, counseling, audio-visuals, workers' meetings, training institutes, leadership classes.

5. Help teachers find comradeship in the task of teaching. The supervisor can begin by being a friendly person who seeks to understand the teacher and to enjoy her as a person worth knowing. The supervisor's relationship with God may help the teacher find needed spiritual companionship. Teachers need this sense of fellowship, and supervisors help provide opportunities where such fellowship may develop.

Workers' meetings may encourage both fellowship and improved teaching. Teachers also need a closer relationship with parents of their pupils than is often obtained, and the supervisors should assist in making parent contacts. Where parent-teacher meetings are the policy of the school, or where parents are consistently enlisted to assume responsibility as they enroll their children, the individual teacher is undergirded by a supporting policy of home and church working together. In any case, the supervisor should assist in working out the best possible home contacts.

Teachers get a sense of fellowship from being a recognized part of some whole-school or whole-church events. Some such events will be dedications of workers, church family nights, the church-school picnic, parents' visiting days, interdepartmental visits, all-church service projects.

6. Give on-the-job assistance. Be ready to help the teachers with their specific problems. Help in advance preparation should always lead to such attitudes as: "When you and the pupils plan together, we may need to see where their suggestions will lead, compare the values of their various suggestions, and work out a new plan of procedure based on your session with them." This gives the expectation of further association of supervisor and teacher, both for evaluation and for further planning. Groups may develop an unexpected need for certain resources, or teachers may unexpectedly have to guide an activity in which they will first need to develop skill.

7. Help teachers evaluate themselves. Modern education knows the value of evaluation in the process of growth. It is the means by which a teacher seeks to understand his strengths and weaknesses so that he can work toward specific and definite changes. This evaluation may be objectified in many ways—by a helpful supervisor, through reading, training classes or conferences of many kinds, using a training type of audio-visuals, visiting other teachers at work, and by the use of objective standards and analyses.

One of the most illusive qualities in self-evaluation is that of self-awareness in which one becomes aware of his own reactions while working in a group and what influence his own reactions have on the group. The teacher needs to know whether his characteristic responses to various kinds of group or individual behavior contribute to or interfere with group progress and growth. What are the teacher's expectations from a group of kindergarten children? What does the teacher expect from a group of primary children? Do teachers know the approximate maturation level of each group and what to expect of the group in the way of abilities, communication, and social relationships? Do teachers know how to help children share their feelings without putting

173

them on the defensive or without talking down to them? Are teachers sensitive to differences in background and needs of individual children?

Studying to understand boys and girls will give teachers a basis on which to explore further the effects of their own teaching, yes, even of their own behavior. But teachers can develop their ability to be self-evaluating only within the context of their relationship with boys and girls. In other words, this is the kind of growth that must take place as one works on the job. An understanding supervisor can help it to take place.

In-Service Training for New Assistants and Young People — The board of Christian education of a local church should constantly hold before its best leaders their privilege and responsibility in developing and training others. Older high-school students and other older young people may serve the vacation church school as assistants to experienced teachers. Inexperienced adults may also learn in this way how to work with groups of children and youth. This in-service training needs careful direction. People can learn poor ways of working as well as good ways so association of trainees should be with the best teachers.

The inexperienced person should be guided in such reading as will help him evaluate what he sees and hears. The experienced leader may need to learn how to help assistants to analyze what is happening to boys and girls and to interpret the values of various group experiences. Experienced leaders let assistants assume increasing responsibilities only as they are able. Such responsibilities should stimulate the experienced teacher to continue to study and grow as he develops in the ability to train others. In-service training thus becomes mutually beneficial as young people and inexperienced adults develop into leaders and experienced teachers. Supplying the church with more leadership is not the least important benefit, but neither is it the only one.

In-service training must always consider what makes a

good experience for the pupil. When young people or even adults without experience first start as helpers, they should assist the leader rather than work with the children and youth. There are many ways of helping leaders—keeping records, preparing materials for use, doing errands for the leader, playing the piano, operating record players or projectors. When the assistant is ready through observation, maturity, and reading to assist with the children, this must be gradually undertaken, carefully guided, and always considered in the light of what is best for the children and youth in the group. They are living human beings, and we must not try to regiment, make over according to a recipe, or mold them into a mental image that we possess. Adults, mature enough to understand both youth and themselves, must learn how to offer opportunity to grow and develop in a nurturing Christian climate.

Other Group Work Experiences— While constantly urged to know their pupils as individuals, church leaders need also to understand how to work with boys and girls in groups. Some vacation church school leadership may be found among men and women who have had experience working with groups, such as Scout leaders, Den mothers, Y.M.C.A. and Y.W.C.A. workers, public-school teachers, playground leaders, and various other kinds of club leaders. These may bring to the vacation church school some training in group leadership. Public-school teachers have been trained to teach and often find an enriching experience in teaching in the vacation church school. As one public-school teacher said, "I teach school all year, but it is nothing like this where the boys and girls are so interested and responsive."

All leaders from other groups need help in discovering and getting acquainted with helpful church-school teaching material. They need to be guided in understanding clearly the purposes of Christian education, and need to see the desirability of democratic teaching methods. All leaders enlisted from other group experiences should be helped to practice their best knowledge of group guidance in Christian education.

The Teacher Prepares to Teach a Unit — 1. Consider one's own pupils, individually and as a group. Do they have needs, interests, and abilities in line with the purposes of this unit? Which purposes need emphasis with these boys and girls? What adaptations of the unit should be made for these pupils? What purposes or activities need to be added for this group?

2. Adequate preparation means studying not only for each coming session but for the whole unit of work and study. Teachers do this with greater insight if they first have some understanding of the purpose and plan back of the whole curriculum so that they can see how the unit they are about to study fits into the whole plan. Some teachers preview the goals of Christian education and note the way the total curriculum provides for a well-rounded, growing experience. Teachers should picture the parts (units) in terms of the whole curriculum. A chart of the lesson materials of the denomination including both Sunday and weekday units of study helps orient the teacher in the curriculum.

3. Read the pupil's material and teacher's textbook for the whole unit of work. This survey should provide an at-homeness with the materials.

4. Consider the purposes to be achieved and for which this material was written. All good teaching materials begin with statements of purpose so that teachers are not just teaching materials, but are helping boys and girls make progress in Christian faith and behavior.

5. Consider the teaching situation—space, time limitations, environment, associations, equipment, other resources, supplies. There must always be adaptations in terms of one's own teaching situation for writers cannot know and write for every local condition. Make the needed adaptations and

collect the available resources that will aid in the use of this unit of study and work.

Before planning procedures a teacher should ask such questions as, "What can the pupils do through which they will make progress toward the purposes set up in this unit?" At this point the teacher does not think so much about what he does to teach as what the pupil does to learn. What will interest the boys and girls so that they set up some goals and purposes for themselves? What might possibly happen in the learning-teaching situation that will result in the pupils striving for new goals, gaining new confidence, achieving a stronger faith, and becoming more Christian in thought and deed? A good textbook should have good suggestions that will guide a teacher at these points and help him make some possible over-all plans.

6. Plan the first session in detail and try to anticipate the plans that will be made by the pupils as they get into the work of the unit so that tentative procedures can be outlined for the following sessions. Remember that changes will come about because of what pupils do in class sessions, the nature of their relationships with one another and the teacher, their thoughts, and the insights they acquire through activities of study, fellowship, worship, and service.

7. Be prepared to evaluate each session before planning the next one, and be prepared to adapt the plans made to changes which grow out of allowing pupils to help in the planning or in making choices of what to do. New teachers can best keep this under control by planning two or three alternatives and allowing pupils to choose, but they should gradually encourage more original planning on the part of the boys and girls.

Summary for Chapters 10 and 11 — The vacation church school can meet problems of enlisting and training leaders in positive ways. The duties and qualifications of leaders must be clearly defined, including those of the director, the vacation church school committee, teachers, assistants, resource persons, secretaries, custodian, recreation leaders, and music directors.

Leaders in the vacation church school should be enlisted through the pulpit, a personnel committee, the regular church-school teachers, and those who are in training classes.

Training leaders for vacation church school may be done through reading and group study, audio-visuals, institutes, workshops, skill shops, laboratory schools, and leadership classes.

Good teaching comes about through careful supervision, helping teachers evaluate their work, and in advance planning for teaching a unit.

Suggestions for Things to Do

1. To recognize a need and to have some ability to meet that need is to be summoned to serve. Many potential leaders should be helped to recognize the needs for service and to discover their abilities to serve. Especially do potential leaders need help in developing these abilities. How can such a program of leadership enlistment and development be carried on in your church?

2. Make out the following lists as you make plans for your vacation church school:

a) tasks that need doing in planning your school and its program

b) qualifications needed by the worker in each task

c) persons with these qualifications, or their potential

d) opportunities which should be provided to prepare these persons to serve

3. Plan a consecration service for all vacation church school leaders (those who plan and those who work in the school). Aim your service at kindling a spirit of enthusiasm, cheerfulness, and dedication.

Values Made Permanent

EVERY EFFORT OF THE CHURCH SHOULD MEET THE TEST OF value. Some people work in the church for the fun they get out of it, but that, too, is a value. That there are values in the vacation church school has been the theme of each preceding chapter. But values can be unclaimed, wasted, or lost. Fruit may be left to rot in orchards instead of being harvested, used, or preserved for future use. Fruits of the vacation church school are rich and can enrich the church life for boys and girls and their parents and teachers. These fruits must be conserved and utilized, or they will be wasted.

Channeling Values Into the Ongoing Church Program— The vacation church school is not a separate organization, agency, or program. At least it is hoped that this is not so. It is the church at work with boys and girls. More specifically, the vacation church school is the church at work with boys and girls during weekdays of the summer, and strives toward the same Christian nurture goals that give direction to other phases of the program during the rest of the church-school year. In other words, the vacation church school is an extension of the church's program into weekdays of the summer. The values of this summer program are closely related to the whole church program, and it is from this viewpoint that we consider ways of making values permanent.

This closing chapter is both a summary and a means of evaluation. The questions suggest what to do at the time of planning, and they offer an objective means of measuring what has been done, as the vacation church school is evaluated both during and after each summer's school. The questions will prove most helpful when more than one person attempts to give the answers. Various viewpoints should be represented, especially at the time of evaluation. Seek evidence to support the answers so that wishful thinking does not intrude. This kind of objective information is needed by the board of Christian education in appraising what has been done, in channeling the values into the ongoing program, and in planning for the next vacation church school.

How Is Pupil Interest Directed? — In what ways do the vacation church school boys and girls show that they are more at home in the church building, program, and fellowship? At-homeness comes from being acquainted and interested and by participating. It also includes a feeling of being welcomed and accepted by others. If the vacation church school is an active time of pupil participation, deeper relationships will be established both among pupils and between pupils and leaders. When vacation church school leaders are not the same as Sunday church-school leaders, there is a need for extending this relationship and developing a loyalty to the rest of the church program. Relationships need to be continued. Special attention should be given to acquainting boys and girls with the whole church family. In what ways are these relationships and activities that establish a common bond of loyalty maintained in your church?

In what ways are the learnings and enthusiasms of the vacation church school being utilized and channeled into the ongoing program of the church? Since both the vacation church school lesson materials and the Sunday church-school lessons contribute to the Christian growth of the same boys and girls, many of the materials of worship and study will have repeated use.

Too often great hymns, prayers, and Scripture passages are not used enough to become familiar to children and youth, and this suggests a contribution the vacation church

180

school can make to the rest of the church program. Many new materials are learned in vacation church school which should be utilized in the Sunday sessions, too. It is well to see that all these learnings are conserved. For example, a passage of Scripture or choral reading learned in the vacation church school may be used in Sunday worship services. How the rest of the church leadership is to be made aware of these new interests and materials should be a matter of joint study and planning.

How Is the Evangelistic Potential Realized? — What efforts were made to find and enroll unchurched boys and girls? The time when the board of Christian education should make provision to interest the unchurched is while planning the vacation church school. Plans would include calls to be made in the homes of prospective pupils and the scheduling of activities to include unchurched families— family picnics or programs in which pupils share with their families and friends. Church members often need to be alerted to their opportunities to show friendliness and extend invitations to their unchurched neighbors. A list of the unchurched boys and girls goes to the pastor and is recorded for use of visitation and cultivation committees for follow-up calls in the homes.

New pupils in the vacation church school should always be considered a responsibility of the church unless it is known that they belong to and are active in another church. Efforts should be made to enlist these pupils in the Sunday church school, the junior choir, and other ongoing activities. How is this being done in your church? Who is responsible? For instance, who discusses with the regular pupils on Sundays, both preceding and during the vacation church school, their opportunity and responsibility for inviting, bringing, and welcoming new pupils to the Sunday program? If the vacation church school builds happy relationships, its members will want to maintain some church group life throughout the year.

181

In a co-operative vacation church school there needs to be community planning to extend the church's outreach. What unchurched areas are there in the community that need a vacation church school, a Sunday church school? What co-operative efforts are the churches making to serve such areas? When the churches meet and plan together to extend their services to unchurched areas, they may conduct a community survey of unchurched families, and they will need to delegate tasks to churches able to follow up the opportunity. Names, addresses, and church preferences of unchurched vacation church school members should be reported to the various churches. In what ways does your church follow up the unchurched for which it is responsible?

How Are Leadership Values Channeled? — Leadership is a precious commodity, and most vacation church schools both develop some new leaders and help others make great forward strides in teaching skills. Every church will want to ask itself what potential new leadership was discovered and what leadership development took place in the vacation church school. In fact, plans should be made in advance to look for new and improved leaders or for persons who show the qualities that are needed in leaders. The following questions will suggest ways in which boards of Christian education may conserve these leadership values:

What records are kept of the various teachers and their special skills and talents?

What systematic approach will be made to conserve these leadership abilities for the entire church program instead of everybody going after that good teacher?

What parents were included as helpers in the vacation church school? Are these listed with the kinds of contributions they are able to make? Who keeps and uses this list?

What resource persons contributed successfully to the program, and how is the record of their contributions made available for future use in the church program?

Since group living has such potential fruitfulness in

Christian teaching, some note should be taken of teachers who are developing skills in guiding group life and in democratic informal procedures that enlist pupil planning, effort, and evaluation. Perhaps the director or supervisor in the vacation church school would be the one to make such a report. Either should be able to give evidences that there was creative teaching and that boys and girls were doing more than repeating facts and memorizing verses. What were the pupils actually learning from the activities in which they were engaged that could be called Christian living? When teachers are found who can get this kind of results, the church will want to plan for new teachers to learn from those who are successful.

Are parents a part of the ongoing program to a greater degree? Where good fellowship is established between teachers and parents, the way may be opened for future relationships in the form of parent-teacher meetings, parents' clubs, or parents' willingness to serve the needs of children as a part of the church-school staff. How will your church take advantage of these opportunities? A foundation for Christian living is laid only as home and church work intelligently and co-operatively toward Christian nurture goals.

If there have been parents and other resource persons participating in the vacation church school, they will now have a better understanding of the Christian nurture needs of the boys and girls to be met both in and out of the church. Parents will have a greater awareness of the purposes and scope of the program of Christian education and of the meaning of teaching. To conserve these values for the whole program of Christian education takes planning. The board of Christian education is responsible for this planning and for the recruiting of these potential new leaders wherever they can best serve. Teachers who use these resource persons and observe their work should be alerted to report on all such persons, giving name, address, phone number, kind of contribution made, to whom made, whether it was on the level of understanding of the group, how it helped the group, how skillfully it was done, and whether the resource persons were able to enlist the interest of the pupils.

The minister as a key leader in the church needs opportunities to meet all the leaders, the boys and girls, the parents, the new people, and the unchurched. It is well to see that the minister is invited to planning meetings, teachers' meetings, and sessions of the vacation church school, and recreational and social activities. It is usually assumed that ministers feel free to attend all such functions whenever they can do so. Better relationships are established when the minister is especially invited to these affairs and when his presence is appreciated and his absence is understood.

What new experiences in training have come to be appreciated by leaders? Planning meetings and work sessions are often held as a means of preparing to teach vacation church school units of work and study. If there is a new interest in such meetings for teaching preparation, it may well spread to other church-school workers if carried over into preparation for Sunday teaching. If a supervisor or director has been largely responsible for training or work sessions, such a leader may be used to give this kind of help regularly or until department superintendents and teachers learn to carry it on themselves. A regular children's division superintendent and a youth division superintendent may be able to function in this way. Even though churches may have a supervisory staff, they sometimes need a demonstration of the effectiveness of such planning meetings. How can such meetings be started in your church as a result of the vacation church school?

How Can the Working Space Be Put to Better Use? — The vacation church school does have access to more of the church building and therefore more room to spread out than Sunday groups do. The longer periods of time and the more informal program of the vacation school also stimulate a more creative use of time and space and equipment. Perhaps this has stirred the imagination toward improvements that ought to be made during the rest of the year. If the same leaders work on Sundays, they will naturally take over some of the improvements where possible. In any event, those evaluating the vacation church school and making a report to the board of Christian education should consider such situations and problems as these:

The vacation church school kindergarten children enjoyed play equipment. Perhaps the Sunday church school has never done so. What provision in space, equipment, and time will be needed to continue such a program on Sundays?

In adjusting the rooms between Sundays and weekdays, the vacation church school teacher prepared the room or space appropriate to the unit being used. How can we help all of our teachers to make their teaching space adequate for good teaching and teach boys and girls to clean up after themselves and return borrowed property?

What new arrangements of furniture encouraged pupil activity and participation? This should be a stimulus for breaking down some formal patterns that handicap informal teaching. Sometimes as a result of the vacation church school it has been found that there should be a new assignment of rooms for the ongoing church-school year. This decision is a responsibility of the board of Christian education. How can it become more conscious of its housing and equipment needs as a result of the vacation church school?

Have Careful Records and Reports Been Made and Used? — When there is adequate provision made for secretarial and clerical help, it is possible to keep accurate and careful records of each pupil. Such records give address, public-school grade, age, and church affiliation of child and parents. Accurate attendance records will yield information about the school as well as about the absent pupils. All records become a part of the permanent files of the church to be used by teachers in guiding pupils, to provide home contacts, and to enlist the family in the church.

185

Records should be kept that summarize the work of the vacation church school. They will provide such data as dates, length of school, textbooks used, and the units taught; the names and addresses of all regular and resource leaders; a listing of all-school activities, such as sharing projects, picnics, family-night programs, closing programs with attendances, and the response to these various activities.

Reports will also be made to the appropriate groups and agencies. Looking back over this chapter one finds many kinds of reports that are to be made to the board of Christian education. Besides the many uses already indicated such reports are to be conserved for use by the next vacation church school committee in its planning for another school.

The board of Christian education does not just bury these reports or lose them in the files, but acts on those that pertain to its functions and reports to the official body of the church and to the general congregation those statistics, findings, and recommendations that have values to these groups. Many of these groups are specialized in their duties so that such questions as these are appropriate:

> What reports should be made to the church cultivation and visitation committee (or evangelism committee), to the finance committee in making next year's budget, to the building and grounds committee, to the leadership-education committee?
>
> How are the total church membership and the community to be made aware of the results of the vacation church school? For instance, reports have values as they are used in publicity items, feature stories with pictures to tell the vacation church school story, and to create an interest.

A good secretary or director of the vacation church school will use the records to report the school to the denominational board of Christian education and to the local or state council of churches.

What New Community Co-operation Has Developed? — Whether the local church conducts its own vacation church school or whether it is conducted by two or more churches, a local committee will profit from an analysis of its co-operative benefits as it answers such questions as these:

1. In preparation for our vacation church school, what help did our leaders get from sources outside our own church? Textbooks are written either denominationally or interdenominationally, so that we immediately begin to find out that we have not worked alone at this job. Training materials are a co-operative venture in most places. Any training schools, clinics, or institutes are usually either denominational or interdenominational.

2. If churches have co-operated either to help train leaders or to conduct the school, what plans for future co-operation should grow out of this experience?

3. Whether or not there has been co-operative or co-ordinated planning for reaching out into all areas of the community with vacation church school privileges, what need exists for joint study and planning? How can our church either help initiate this or participate in such planning?

The Beginning and the End — The pages of this book are dedicated not so much to the vacation church school as to boys and girls for whose Christian nurture we are responsible. The living needs of living boys and girls become our great concern as we work with them in and through the church. To this end we provide good vacation church schools. The great question we must ask ourselves—the question basic to all others that have been listed here— is what will achieve within and for boys and girls that kind of living for which Jesus said, "I came that they may have life, and have it abundantly" (John 10:10). Let us test both our vacation church schools and ourselves by this great purpose.

187

Bibliography

THIS BIBLIOGRAPHY IS CONFINED TO SELECTED BOOKS AND manuals concerned with principles and practices of value to administrators of vacation church schools. Such books make possible a further study of topics dealt with in these chapters. The comments, and in many cases the titles, suggest the area of study.

Many denominational resource books and the many vacation church school textbooks are not listed here as such lists are revised annually and made available to church leaders through denominational and interdenominational publishing agencies. The leader's personal growth and enrichment, his need of Bible study, and a growing understanding of the meaning of the Christian faith are a part of every leader's training in Christian education. This training should be continued, but this bibliography does not fulfill that purpose as most good vacation church school teaching materials suggest such reading for the leader.

There are four sections to the bibliography. The introductory section is called "Background," and the last three sections follow the three parts of the book.

Background

Books giving a basic understanding of education and/or Christian education, with suggestions for principles and practices:

Applegate, Mauree. *Everybody's Business—Our Children*. Evanston, Ill.: Row, Peterson & Co., 1952.
When we understand what children need, it will make a difference in how we teach.
Creating a Good Environment for Learning. 1954 Yearbook of the

188

Association for Supervision and Curriculum Development. Washington, D. C.: National Education Association.
  Creating learning conditions and environment for good teaching.
Havighurst, Robert J. *Developmental Tasks and Education.* New York: Longmans, Green & Co., Inc., 1952.
  There is a teachable moment, a time that is ripe for learning certain tasks.
Macomber, Freeman Glenn. *Principles of Teaching in the Elementary School.* New York: American Book Company, 1954.
  Clarifies the differences between conventional and modern teaching, clearly indicates what is meant by experience units and how to guide such teaching.
Mort, Paul R., and Vincent, W. S. *Modern Educational Practice.* New York: McGraw-Hill Book Co., Inc., 1950.
  Very readable and ably supported by psychology and the demands of living.
Murray, Albert V. *Education Into Religion.* New York: Harper & Bro., 1953.
  Toward a basic understanding of Christian education.
Schisler, J. Q. *Christian Teaching in the Churches.* New York and Nashville: Abingdon Press, 1954.
  A sound presentation of a helpful program of Christian education in local churches.
Sherrill, Lewis J. *The Gift of Power.* New York: The Macmillan Co., 1955.
  A modern philosophy of Christian education.
Wyckoff, D. Campbell. *The Task of Christian Education.* Philadelphia: Westminster Press, 1955.
  A guide for Christian educators in getting acquainted with their task and carrying it on.

Part I. The Vacation Church School Picture

The nature and program of the vacation church school as related to understanding the various age groups and their experiences are given in the following books:

Cunningham, Ruth, et al. *Understanding Group Behavior of Boys and Girls.* New York: Teachers College, Columbia University, 1951.
Hartley, R. E., et al. *Understanding Children's Play.* New York: Columbia University Press, 1952.
Jenkins, G. G., et al. *These Are Your Children.* Chicago: Albert Whitman & Co., 1949.
  A very readable volume which helps in understanding how children develop and how to guide them.

Heffernan, Helen (editor). *Guiding the Young Children*. Boston: D. C. Heath & Co., 1951.
> A chance to meet the five-year-old and his teacher in some first-hand accounts.

Wills, Clarice, and Stegeman, William. *Living in the Kindergarten*. Chicago: Follett Publishing Co., 1950.
> Some good, recent ideas for teaching four- and five-year-old children in public-school kindergartens which would help vacation church school teachers.

Heron, Frances Dunlap. *Kathy Ann, Kindergartner*. New York and Nashville: Abingdon Press, 1955.
> A delightful book revealing Sunday school as it appears to a five-year-old.

Shields, Elizabeth McE. *Guiding Kindergarten Children in the Church School*. Rev. 1955 Dorothea G. Mallard. Richmond, Va.: John Knox Press.
> Suggests ways of working with four- and five-year-old children at church.

Roorbach, Rosemary K. *Religion in the Kindergarten*. New York: Harper & Bro., 1949.
> Methods and procedures for work with children in through-the-week kindergarten in the church.

Smither, Ethel. *Primary Children Learn at Church*. New York and Nashville: Abingdon Press, 1944.
> The use of methods, materials, and equipment in guiding primary children at church.

Hill, Dorothy LaCroix. *Working With Juniors at Church*. New York and Nashville: Abingdon Press, 1955.
> Practical and suggestive guidance in working with juniors.

Griffiths, Louise B. *The Teacher and Young Teens*. St. Louis: The Bethany Press, 1954.
> For all adult workers with twelve- to fourteen-year-olds, this book stresses characteristics and needs of early teen-agers and gives guidance in meeting these needs and in developing more effective ways of teaching.

Brown, Jeanette Perkins. *The Storyteller in Religious Education*. Boston: Pilgrim Press, 1951.
> A guide to teachers in the preparation and telling of stories.

Shields, Elizabeth McE. *Music in the Religious Growth of Children*. New York and Nashville: Abingdon Press, 1943.
> How to use music to enrich the child's religious living.

Thomas, Edith Lovell. *Music in Christian Education*. New York and Nashville: Abingdon Press, 1953.
> The place of music in Christian education with many suggested experiences.

Morsch, Vivian Sharp. *The Use of Music in Christian Education*. Philadelphia: The Westminster Press, 1956.
> Gives practical guidance in using music in every phase of the program of the church.

Ward, Winifred. *Playmaking With Children*. New York: Appleton-Century-Crofts, Inc., 1947.
> A guide to creative dramatics from kindergarten to high school.

Welker, Edith. *Friends With All the World*. New York: Friendship Press, 1954.
> Helpful suggestions for vacation church schools in missionary education.

Part II. The Vacation Church School Belongs

Many of the following books might well be included in the first section but are listed here because of their bearing on the above emphases:

Gable, Lee J. *Christian Nurture Through the Church*. New York: National Council of the Churches of Christ in the U.S.A., 1955.
> Special attention is called to chapters 1 to 4 on the church and families, and chapters 10 and 11 for community relationships.

Fallaw, Wesner. *The Modern Parent and the Teaching Church*. New York: The Macmillan Co., 1946.
> A study of the co-operation of the church and home in the Christian education of the family.

Hymes, James L., Jr., *Effective Home-School Relations*. New York: Prentice-Hall, Inc., 1953.
> A book of practical principles and practices in effective home-school co-operation.

Jones, Mary Alice. *Guiding Children in Christian Growth*. New York and Nashville: Abingdon Press, 1949.
> Special attention is called to chapters 3 and 4, "Learning Through Fellowship—in the Family and in the Church."

Lotz, Philip Henry (editor). *Orientation in Religious Education*. New York and Nashville: Abingdon Press, 1950.
> Special attention is called to chapter 26, "The Community as a Unit of Religious Education" by Helen Marie Edick.

Munro, Harry C. *Protestant Nurture*. New York: Prentice-Hall, Inc., 1956.
> An over-all view of the church's educational task that contains a very significant statement concerning family responsibility (pages 232, 241) and the religious community (page 254).

Vieth, Paul (editor). *The Church and Christian Education*. St. Louis: Bethany Press, 1947.

A sound philosophy in dealing with the community and the church.

Part III. Planning and Administration

The How of the Vacation Church School
Basic Briefs for Vacation Church School
Developing Vacation Church School Leadership
Manuals from the Division of Christian Education of the National Council of the Churches of Christ in the U.S.A.

Frank, Lawrence K. *How to Be a Modern Leader*. New York: Association Press, 1954.

Practical suggestions for leadership.
Gable, Lee. *Christian Nurture Through the Church*. New York: National Council of the Churches of Christ in the U.S.A., 1955.

Helpful suggestions for enlisting and training leaders are in chapter 4. Other administrative problems are in chapters 4 to 12.
Gwynn, Price H. *Leadership Education in the Local Church*. Philadelphia: Westminster Press, 1952.

A comprehensive guide to the training of teachers and other leaders.
McKibben, Frank M. *Guiding Workers in Christian Education*. New York and Nashville: Abingdon Press, 1953.

Practical suggestions for developing leadership.
Miller, Randolph Crump. *Education for Christian Living*. Prentice-Hall, Inc., 1956.

See especially Part IV, Administration of Religious Education.
Powell, R. R. *Improving Your Church School*. New York and Nashville: Abingdon Press, 1949.

Practical suggestions to help make church-school teaching effective.
Tower, Howard E. *Church Use of Audio-Visuals*. New York and Nashville: Abingdon Press, 1951.

Basic principles and methods for the use of audio-visual resources.